D1134498

Editor's Letter

Hello and welcome to the *Woman's Weekly* Yearbook 2014, a new way for you to enjoy all the brilliant content of the magazine every day of the year, with the added bonus of a diary for each week to make it even more invaluable (don't forget to buy the magazine every Wednesday!). We've compiled a wonderful selection of the most popular parts of the magazine, so there are tasty recipes, gorgeous knitting patterns and delightful craft makes, plus useful health advice and our readers' recommendations of enchanting places to visit. And for those moments when you can put your feet up with a nice cuppa, there are entertaining fiction stories and brain-teasing puzzles.

I hope you will be entertained, informed and inspired by everything and I wish you all a very good year.

Diane Kenwood
EDITOR, *WOMAN'S WEEKLY*

Published 2013.
Pedigree Books Limited, Beech Hill House, Walnut Gardens, Exeter, Devon EX4 4DH
www.pedigreebooks.com | books@pedigreegroup.co.uk
The Pedigree trademark, email and website addresses, are the sole and exclusive properties of Pedigree Group Limited, used under licence in this publication.

Compiled and edited by Diane Kenwood
Designed by Sofia Bakhsh
Sub-edited by Rebecca Smith

Special thanks to the readers and contibutors of **Woman's Weekly** magazine, who have assisted with the compilation of this Yearbook.

Contents

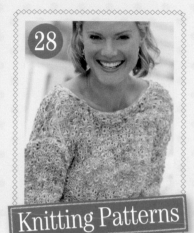

Knitting Patterns

28

Craft Makes

62

Recipes

78

JANUARY

30 Dec, 2013

31 Dec, 2013

1 Wednesday BANK HOLIDAY

2 Thursday

3 Friday

4 Saturday

5 Sunday

Lilac And Lace

A simple lace pattern gives this knit its feminine style — combine it with a soft pastel shade and you're set for summer!

MEASUREMENTS
To fit sizes 81-86 (91-97) (102-107) cm/32-34 (36-38) (40-42) in.
Actual measurements 99 (112.5) (126) cm/39 (44¼) (49½) in.
Side seam (excluding armbands) 36 (38) (40) cm/14 (15) (15¾) in.
Length to shoulder 56 (60) (64) cm/22 (23½) (25¼) in.

MATERIALS
6 (7) (8) 50g balls of Rowan 4-ply Cotton. No. 9 (3¾ mm) knitting needles. Yarn costs about £3.35 per 50g ball. We used Provence (139). For stockists, write to: Rowan Yarns, Green Lane Mill, Holmfirth, West Yorkshire HD9 2DX (01484 681881).

TENSION
27 stitches and 30 rows, to 10 x 10cm over pattern, using No. 9 (3¾mm) needles.

ABBREVIATIONS
K, knit; **p,** purl; **st,** stitch; **sl,** slip; **tog,** together; **dec,** decrease (by taking 2 sts tog); **psso,** pass sl st over; **skpo,** (sl1, k1, psso); **up1,** pick up loop lying between needles and k into back of it; **yf,** yarn forward to make a st.

NOTE
Instructions are given for small size. Where they vary, work figures in round brackets for larger sizes. Instructions in square brackets are worked as stated after 2nd bracket.

BACK

With No. 9 (3¾mm) needles, cast on loosely 134 (152) (170) sts.
P 1 row.
Work pattern thus: **1st row:** K14, [yf, k1, yf, k3, sl1, k2tog, psso, k11] to last 12 sts, yf, k1, yf, k3, sl1, k2tog, psso, k5.
2nd row and following alternate rows: P.
3rd row: K15, [yf, k1, yf, k2, sl1, k2tog, psso, k12] to last 11 sts, yf, k1, yf, k2, sl1, k2tog, psso, k5.
5th row: K5, [k3tog, k4, yf, k1, yf, k3, yf, k1, yf, k1, sl1, k2tog, psso, k2] to last 21 sts, k3tog, k4, yf, k1, yf, k3, [yf, k1] twice, sl1, k2tog, psso, k5.
7th row: K5, [k3tog, k3, yf, k1, yf, k11] to last 21 sts, k3tog, k3, yf, k1, yf, k14.
9th row: K5, [k3tog, k2, yf, k1, yf, k12] to last 21 sts, k3tog, k2, yf, k1, yf, k15.
11th row: K5, [k3tog, k1, yf, k1, yf, k3, yf, k1, yf, k4, sl1, k2tog, psso, k2] to last 21 sts, k3tog, k1, yf, k1, yf, k3, yf, k1, yf, k4, sl1, k2tog, psso, k5.
12th row: P.
These 12 rows form pattern.
Pattern another 6 rows.
Shape sides: Dec row: K1, k2tog, pattern to last 3 sts, skpo, k1.
Pattern 9 rows.
Repeat last 10 rows, twice more, then dec row again — 126 (144) (162) sts.
Pattern another 11 (11) (15) rows.
Increase row: K1, up1, pattern to last st, up1, k1.
Pattern 9 (11) (11) rows.
Repeat last 10 (1a) (12) rows, twice more, then increase row again — 134 (152) (170) sts.
Pattern another 17 (17) (19) rows.
Shape armholes: Keeping pattern correct, cast off loosely 7 (8) (9) sts at beginning of next 2 rows.
Dec 1 st at each end of next 9 (13) (13) rows and 5 (7) (8) following alternate rows — 92 (96) (110) sts. **
Pattern another 33 (31) (35) rows.
Shape neck: Next row: Pattern 35 (37) (44), turn and work on these sts only for right side neck.
Right side neck: Cast off 6 (6) (7) sts at beginning of next row and 2 following alternate rows.
Cast off remaining 17 (19) (23) sts for shoulder.
Left side neck: With right side facing, rejoin yarn to remaining sts, cast off next 22 sts, pattern to end. Pattern 1 row. Cast off 6 (6) (7) sts at beginning of next row and 2 following alternate rows.
Cast off remaining 17 (19) (23) sts for shoulder.

FRONT

Work as back to **.
Pattern another 21 (19) (23) rows.
Shape neck: Next row: Pattern 38 (40) (47), turn and work on these sts only for left side neck.
Left side neck: Cast off 4 (4) (5) sts at beginning of next row and 2 following alternate rows and 3 sts on 3 following alternate rows — 17 (19) (23) sts. Pattern another 6 rows. Cast off remaining sts for shoulder.
Right side neck: With right side facing, rejoin yarn to remaining sts, cast off next 16 sts, pattern to end. Pattern 1 row. Cast off 4 (4) (5) sts at beginning of next row and 2 following alternate rows and 3 sts on 3 following alternate rows — 17 (19) (23) sts. Pattern another 6 rows. Cast off remaining sts for shoulder.

BACK COLLAR

With No. 9 (3¾mm) needles, cast on loosely 92 sts.
P 1 row.

Work pattern thus: **1st row:** K11, [yf, k1, yf, k3, sl1, k2tog, psso, k11] to last 9 sts, yf, k1, yf, k3, sl1, k2tog, psso, k2.
2nd row and following alternate rows: P.
3rd row: K12, [yf, k1, yf, k2, sl1, k2tog, psso, k12] to last 8 sts, yf, k1, yf, k2, sl1, k2tog, psso, k2.
5th row: K2, [k3tog, k4, yf, k1, yf, k3, yf, k1, yf, k1, sl1, k2tog, psso, k2] to end.
7th row: K2, [k3tog, k3, yf, k1, yf, k11] to end.
9th row: K2, [k3tog, k2, yf, k1, yf, k12] to end.
11th row: K2, [k3tog, k1, yf, k1, yf, k3, yf, k1, yf, k4, sl1, k2tog, psso, k2] to end.
12th row: P.
These 12 rows form pattern. Pattern another 42 rows. Cast off loosely.

FRONT COLLAR

With No. 9 (3¾mm) needles, cast on 128 sts. P 1 row.
Work 54 rows in pattern as given for back collar. Cast off loosely.

ARMBANDS

(BOTH ALIKE)
Join shoulder seams. With right side facing and using No. 9 (3¾mm) needles, pick up and k112 (122) (132) sts evenly around armhole edge. K 2 rows. Cast off kwise.

TO MAKE UP

Press as given on ball band. Join row-ends of front and back collar pieces together at each end. With right side of collar to wrong side of top, oversew collar to neck edge, easing in fullness to fit. Join side seams, including armbands.

This sleeveless top has shaped sides and a scooped neck with a large cowl collar. It's knitted in an all-over lace stitch with garter-stitch armbands. The yarn is pure cotton.

Marlborough in Wiltshire

POST – CARD

Reader Esther Newton, from Thatcham, Berkshire, nominates Marlborough in Wiltshire

'I used to have a very stressful job, but when my mum, dad and I had a day out in Marlborough, all my stresses faded away — especially after tea in an excellent tea room. This pretty town is such a beautiful, tranquil place, you can't help but feel calm. Now, when I visit with my own daughter, it brings back warm, happy memories.'

Malham in North Yorkshire

POST – CARD

Reader Sheila Hall, from Halifax, West Yorkshire, chooses Malham, North Yorkshire

'I love to have a trip up into the Dales and, for me, there's nowhere nicer than Malham with its marvellous scenery and wide-open spaces. We always head for the Cove and have a bracing walk up the steps for the terrific view, then drive up to the Tarn to spot any wildlife. It's the best day out for me!'

6 Monday

7 Tuesday

8 Wednesday

9 Thursday

10 Friday

11 Saturday

12 Sunday

Citrus Roasted Chicken

SERVES *4-6*
CALORIES *200*
FAT *9g*
SATURATED FAT *2g*
SUITABLE FOR FREEZING *Yes*

INGREDIENTS

* *4 tablespoons marmalade (preferably clementine marmalade)*
* *2 tablespoons olive oil*
* *1 tablespoon Dijon mustard*
* *1 clove garlic, peeled and crushed*
* *1 level tablespoon freshly grated ginger*
* *Salt and freshly ground black pepper*
* *8-12 chicken thighs and/or drumsticks*
* *4-6 clementines, or tangerines*
* *1-2 tablespoons chopped fresh parsley*

1 Preheat the oven to 200°C or Gas Mark 6. In a large bowl, mix together the marmalade, olive oil, mustard, garlic, ginger and seasoning.

2 Slash the chicken skin diagonally 3 times in each thigh/drumstick. Add the chicken to the bowl and coat it in the marmalade mixture.

3 Spread the chicken pieces out in a large roasting tin and pour over any of the marmalade juices in the bowl.

4 Thinly slice the clementines, or tangerines, and place over the chicken pieces, pressing some in between the pieces.

5 Cover the roasting tin with foil and place in the centre of the oven. Bake for 20 minutes, then remove foil and bake for a further 30-40 minutes, basting occasionally, until the chicken is starting to turn golden and the juices run clear when the flesh is pierced. Remove from the oven and sprinkle parsley over before serving.

TIP FROM OUR KITCHEN

The cooled chicken can be packed in a suitable container and frozen for up to 1 month. Allow it to defrost before thoroughly reheating.

Your Good Health

Ask Dr Mel

Q I often feel dizzy for a few seconds when tilting my head or turning over in bed. Can anything be done?

A This sounds like benign positional vertigo (BPV), a disorder of the inner ear that can be a real nuisance. Each of our ears has three fluid-filled semicircular canals that contain tiny hairs and gritty otoliths that detect head movement; these tell our brains "where we are". It's thought that detached otoliths may float around like tealeaves, contradicting other messages that tell the brain when the head has stopped moving.

BPV often starts in mid-life, and affects more women than men. It may be due to "wear and tear" but can be triggered by a bang on the head, viruses or ear disease. The vertigo (moving feeling) starts a few seconds after the head moves and lasts up to half a minute, usually without nausea.

The Hallpike test (a careful neck movement) can be used to diagnose BPV; you may need to see a specialist and have an MR scan to rule out other causes of vertigo. BPV often settles by itself; if not, the specialist may carry out a head-repositioning treatment called the Epley manoeuvre, which could well relieve symptoms.

TRY THIS — Rebounding

When you're recovering from cold or flu, you need to start exercising again slowly. A walk is ideal, but if it's freezing outside and you want to avoid catching a chill, then a mini-trampoline (rebounder) is a perfect alternative. It will boost your immune system, as well as being kind to your joints, and an energetic rebounding session can be as beneficial as a 3km walk.

HEALTH ON MY SHELF
Kate Moorby, physiotherapist

What's in your medicine cabinet?
Effervescent vitamin C and the ingredients to make a whisky-based hot toddy.
What's good in your fridge?
Yogurt with friendly bacteria.
What's your favourite exercise?
Spin classes with a good background of dance music to keep me going.
What's a special treat?
Liquorice Catherine wheels from my local sweet shop.
What makes you happy?
Many things, but especially the excited giggles of my small nieces and nephews.
Any major health scare or wake-up call?
I was shocked when blood tests showed that, despite my petite build, I had high cholesterol. I've since cut back on the eclairs.
What stresses you out?
Being late for a flight.
Any childhood remedies you still use?
Kissing it better.

TAKE 5...
Reasons for feeling cold

1 FEVER DUE TO INFECTION — causes "chills" and makes you "hot and cold" by turns.

2 POOR CIRCULATION IN HANDS AND FEET — caused by narrowed arteries (arteriosclerosis) or beta-blocker drugs used to treat angina and raised blood pressure.

3 RAYNAUD'S PHENOMENON — cold exposure constricts surface blood vessels, so skin turns white, then blue, then red. Sometimes linked to arthritic conditions.

4 HYPOTHERMIA — you'll shiver if your body temperature drops; dangerously low temperatures can lead to coma.

5 SHOCK — for example, caused by blood loss or heart problems, will make you feel shivery.

13 Monday

14 Tuesday

15 Wednesday

16 Thursday

17 Friday

18 Saturday

19 Sunday

Take A Book

Transform a plain diary, notebook or album into something special that you'll be proud to leave on show

Desk Diary

Use wrapping paper to brighten up a dull diary.

YOU WILL NEED
* Plain A4 diary
* Wrapping paper — we used Cavallini paper, £3.25 (0117 924 7302; www.papernation.co.uk)
* 35cm length of 2cm-wide velvet ribbon
* Bag charm
* Small lace or ribbon bow
* Double-sided tape
* PVA glue
* Needle and thread
* Small pair of paper scissors

Stationery, from a selection at Paperchase (020 7467 6200; www.paperchase.co.uk)

1 Open the diary out flat and lay it cover-side down on top of the wrong side of the wrapping paper. Draw lightly around the outer edges of the book, ensuring that the spine is flat on the paper. Add a 1.5cm margin all the way round and cut the shape out.

2 Stick a strip of double-sided tape down the spine of the diary and all around the outer edges of the inside covers. Peel the backing paper from the double-sided tape on the spine and spread PVA glue sparingly over the front and back covers of the diary. Carefully lay the book, cover-side down, in the centre of the piece of wrapping paper, spine first. Gently smooth the wrapping paper down over the front and back.

3 Mitre the corners of the wrapping paper at 45 degrees and cut a triangular shape at the top and bottom of the spine to remove unwanted bulk. Then fold excess paper over to the inside covers of the diary. Peel the backing paper from the tape and press paper edges in place to secure them.

4 Stitch one end of the velvet ribbon to the top of the existing dividing ribbon from your diary. Trim the original ribbon and tuck any excess into the spine. Loop the other end of the ribbon through your chosen bag charm and stitch it firmly in place. Cover stitching with a delicate lace bow.

NOW TRY THESE...

Here are some more ideas to create your own lovely book covers.
* Gardening journal covered with images from colourful seed packets.
* Wedding album covered with cream silk and finished with two overlapping wire hearts.
* Recipe book covered in wipeable oilcloth.
* Holiday scrapbook covered with holiday snapshots.
* Christening album covered in pink or blue with a pair of baby bootees cut out from paper.

Travel Journal

Use clever collage to make your memoirs even brighter.

YOU WILL NEED
* Notebook
* Base paper of your choice (we used a map design)
* Stamps, letters, tickets brochures, etc, for collage
* Japanese washi tape
* PVA glue
* Scissors

London map wrapping paper, £3.25 per sheet; Japanese washi masking tape, ref. 00491764, £4.25, both Paperchase (details as before)

1 Place notebook cover-side down on the wrong side of your chosen base paper. We used map-themed wrapping paper, but any patterned good-quality paper will do just as well. Draw lightly around the cover and cut shape out, trimming it to fit flush with the spine tape. Glue the paper in place with PVA glue.

2 Then arrange your collage pieces on top of the paper. We used a strip of washi (Japanese masking) tape next to the spine tape, then added cut out shapes from pieces of wrapping paper, old stamps, tickets, labels, airmail letters, brochures and airmail stickers. You could also add photos or bits of postcards, if desired.

3 When you are happy with your arrangement, glue all the bits firmly in place. Allow the glue to dry thoroughly before use.

Fabric-covered Album

Co-ordinate your album with your home furnishings.

1 Cover your album using the instructions for the diary, opposite, but replacing the paper with your chosen fabric and using fabric glue instead of PVA.

2 To prevent fraying, treat all of the raw edges of the fabric with either Fraycheck or glue after cutting out the cover.

3 Omit step 4 from the diary instructions and, instead, make ties by cutting two 30cm lengths of ribbon and gluing them just inside the front and back covers, halfway up the edge. Leave to dry and tie in a bow.

TIPS
✓ Avoid using a heavy fabric or one with a thick, raised design, as this will be too bulk at the corners.
✓ Spread the fabric glue thinly, so that it doesn't bleed through to the right side of the fabric.

YOU WILL NEED
* Plain photo album
* Fabric of your choice (see tips, above)
* Fabric glue or Fraycheck
* Double-sided tape
* 30cm length of 2cm-wide ribbon
* Scissors

The balcony

I hadn't quarrelled with my husband. That hadn't been the problem at all. We'd just stopped talking altogether...

"*Pronto. Buongiorno... Si...Si, va bene... Si, capisco... Grazie... A domani... Ciao.*"

I grinned and did a little dance. If they'd called me back, it meant they were hiring and if they were hiring, it meant I'd get a job and if I got a job, it meant the Big Idea was going to work and we could stay here.

I sat down with a sigh on the elegant little chair, its metal back worked in curves and curlicues, and put my mobile on the breakfast table with its blue and white checked cloth. Smiling out over the window boxes, I looked at the view from the balcony.

I had to admit, it wasn't quite what I'd expected. I thought I'd be able to see the Adriatic, three hundred metres away, through the pine trees, but all I could see was the garden and the dusty, rutted track that led away from the road and threaded between the villas and condominiums, and I could see an apartment building on the other side of the track. I'd heard a couple quarrelling there the day before.

I hadn't quarrelled with my husband. That hadn't been the problem at all — quite the opposite. We'd just stopped talking altogether. It wasn't the worst way to end a marriage, probably, but it was an ending just the same.

There were pine trees in the garden. I could reach out and touch one from the balcony. It had springy tufts of lime green needles longer than my fingers. Overnight, the trees seemed to shed their old, dead, brown needles because there were always some on the balcony in the morning. That and the little, sticky, clear blobs of resin that sat like raindrops on the handrail but didn't dry away in the warm Italian sun.

The day before, I'd come out through the French doors and almost stepped on a strange green bug, lying on its back on the tiles, waving its legs in the air and totally unable to right itself. The sun was hot, even that early in the morning, even in the partial shade of the pines and the stripy awning. The bug wouldn't last long like that.

I pressed my hand flat on the floor beside it. I thought it maybe wouldn't take the risk of climbing onto a human but it was too desperate to be picky. I didn't

The idea had been born. It was big and beautiful

even feel its pedalling feet as it found a purchase on my skin and clambered on, righting itself in the process. The bug was the size of my thumbnail and pretty much the same shape. It was the strangest thing. I took him to the edge of the balcony and let him climb onto the long, safe needles of the pine tree. I watched him for a while as he ambled along a twig.

He. I was calling him "he". I had a lot of empathy with that bug. There he was, helpless, staring at a future as empty as the sky, going nowhere. I knew how that felt. I'd known for a long time, ever since my marriage ended. No. It was a lot longer, now I came to think about it. Years and years.

And then, one afternoon, over a friend's brightly cluttered kitchen table, The Idea had been born. It was big and beautiful and quite, quite mad. "Go to Italy," it said. "You know you've always wanted to. Rent out the house, quit your job, take the children and go to Italy. Find work. Stay there for a year. See Venice and the Trevi Fountain and the Leaning Tower of Pisa. Go on!"

Straight away I thought, 'Oooh, I can't do that! I can't possibly do that!' And then I thought about it some more, over ever-so-English tea and cake and the surreal enormity of my friend's water bill. And I stopped thinking sanely and I thought, 'Actually...I can.'

I resigned from work. They told me how sorry they'd be to see me go but how excited they were by my big adventure. The start of great things. They threw me a party and made me give a speech.

I told all my friends. They invited me over for dinner and plied me with wine and promised to visit me in Italy. The Orient Express, I told them, goes to Venice...

And I was here. I was really here. In Italy. By the Adriatic, even if I couldn't see it. Eating breakfast on the balcony. There were oleanders in the garden with flowers the colour of cooked salmon and long, dark, strap-like leaves. The sun was hot and the shade was cool and the warm air I was breathing was Italian air and the cool water I was drinking was Italian water and I'd done it. I'd taken a risk and righted myself in the process. And now I was ambling towards a future. True, I didn't know what it held, but I didn't have to. It was there, like the Adriatic. And you can't always expect a view, even from a balcony.

THE END

© Margaret Rowe, 2010

20 Monday

21 Tuesday

22 Wednesday

23 Thursday

24 Friday

25 Saturday

26 Sunday

SPIRAL CROSSWORD

Just enter your solutions clockwise into the grid, starting from top left. You'll know how many letters are in each by the position on the grid where each new clue begins. But there are no intersecting letters to help you — so concentrate to complete the spiral.

CLUES

1 Finished

2 Succeed, get on (2 words)

3 Heavy-footed

4 Scary fairground ride (2 words)

5 Chilly or quick

6 Fresh-faced

7 Match between two teams from the same area (2 words)

8 Opposite of 'mine'

9 Doodle or write untidily

10 Fair, impartial (hyphenated)

11 ___ Goodrem, Aussie singer and actress

12 ___ and Eve, Bible's first people

13 Glossy publication

14 Outside of a house

15 Furry pet kept in a hutch

16 Brand names

17 Sugary additive

18 Standard (procedure)

19 Accurate, precise

20 One of two identical people

21 Garment worn in bed

22 Of sailors, marine

23 Game of jumping over each other

24 Father's mother

25 Dried (clothes) in a machine

26 Nasty, unpleasant

27 Take advantage of

28 Shake from fear or cold

29 Make certain

30 Written school assignment

31 Sing like a Tyrolean mountaineer

32 Faithfulness

33 Footballer's warning (2 words)

34 Trader

35 Lines (of seats)

36 Organised trip to observe wild animals in East Africa

LINKWORDS

Fit six words into the grid so that each links with the end of the word on its left and the beginning of the one on its right. Then unscramble the letters in the shaded squares to make a word.
CLUE Large country (6).

OFFICIAL						PASSAGE
UNSKILLED						CAMP
LEGAL						MERCIES
MARKET						DANCE
FACE						KEG
TIME						AGENCY

Solutions to this months puzzle on next months puzzle

SOLUTIONS FOR DECEMBER, 2014

ACROSS: 12 Savings account **13** Upheaval **14** Chic **15** Lodging **16** Marvellous **17** Attic **19** Grief **20** Pounds **22** Deaf **25** War-torn **26** At the last minute **29** Snowy owl **30** Static **31** Smart **34** Remove **36** Kindliest **38** Recent **39** Offer **40** Jargon **41** Instinct **45** Compliments slip **46** Phone-in **47** Stay **48** Easter **50** Stale **52** Anger **55** Distribute **58** Brosnan **59** Rack **61** Seedbeds **62** Inverted commas
DOWN: 1 Lash **2** Biscuit tin **3** Agile **4** Warder **5** Accidental **6** Lunge **7** Item **8** Fun run **9** Threesome **10** Mall **11** Manufacturing **18** Tray **21** On leave **22** Dynamic **23** Trawler **24** Ghostliness **27** Swiftest **28** Workmate **32** Self-contained **33** Freight **35** Overpay **37** Nightie **41** Idiot board **42** Conundrums **43** Sidelines **44** Live **49** Squash **51** Linger **53** Above **54** Knock **56** Tide **57** Emit **60** Crag
SNOOKER

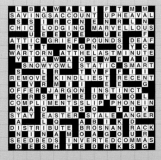

27 Monday

28 Tuesday

29 Wednesday

30 Thursday

31 Friday

1 Saturday

2 Sunday

FEBRUARY

3 Monday

4 Tuesday

5 Wednesday

6 Thursday

7 Friday

8 Saturday

9 Sunday

Give ~~Have~~ a heart

Affectionate gifts for you to create and give to a loved one for Valentine's Day (or any time!)

The Soft Touch

Red-and-white striped fabric, £12 per metre; super-soft toy filler, £4.50 per 250g bag, both John Lewis (0845 604 9049; www.johnlewis.com). Red-stitched ribbon, £1 per metre, Jane Means (01522 522544; www.janemeans. co.uk)

Cut out two fabric hearts, using the largest template, left (1: enlarge it by 200% on a photocopier first). Sew the hearts together with right sides facing, and an 8mm seam allowance. Machine-stitch with a straight stitch or hand-sew with a backstitch all around, leaving a 2cm opening on one long side. Using needlework scissors, snip into the seam allowance at 1cm intervals to make it easier to turn the heart through and give a cleaner finish. Turn it right side out and stuff with soft toy filling. Use small pieces and pack it quite loosely, so the heart remains soft.

Once it's filled, hand-stitch the opening closed. Cut a 24cm length of ribbon and loop it in half, so the cut ends cross over. Pin to the heart and secure with a few stitches, then sew a button onto the point where the ribbon crosses.

Templates 1-4 (enlarge all the hearts by 200% on a photocopier)

Drink To Me Only

Create heart transfers using Magic Decal Paper and give your plain coffee or tea set a romantic touch.

First, print a page of red colour onto Magic Decal Paper. Do this using a colour photocopier or laserjet printer at your local print shop.

Using the templates (opposite), enlarged by 200%, cut out the larger red heart (2) for the coffee pot and four of the smallest red hearts (4) for the cups, from the paper. Wet the face side of the motif until the film slides away, then dampen the pot where you want it to go. Submerge the motif in water for 10 seconds and then place it face down on the pot, paper side facing outwards. Peel off backing paper and smooth out any bubbles. Put in the oven for up to 10 minutes at 180°C or Gas Mark 4. Submerge the pot in cold water for 3-5 minutes and peel off the top film. Repeat the process for the cups.

Coffee pot, £5; espresso cup and saucer, £2.50 each, all Wilkinson (0845 608 0807; www.wilkinsonplus.com). Magic Decal Paper, £3.25 per sheet, Crafty Computer Paper (0116 274 4755; www.craftycomputerpaper.co.uk). Alessi Big Love Heart espresso spoons, £19.50 for a set of four, John Lewis (details as before). Valentine cupcakes, from a selection at Storm In A Cupcake (07906 009129; www.storminacupcake.com)

Romantic Read

Double-sided sticky tape, £4.29, Hobbycraft (0845 051 6599; www.hobbycraft.co.uk). A5 'With Love' Me to You Bear Double-sided Paper Pack, £4, Me To You (01268 288691; www.metoyouonline.com)

Send a card that's a bookmark, too. Using the templates (opposite), enlarged by 200%, cut a smaller heart (3) from patterned card and a larger heart (2) in plain red. Place a strip of double-sided sticky tape on the top half of the reverse side of the smaller one. Peel off the tape's backing and stick smaller heart centrally onto the larger heart.

Your Good Health

Ask Dr Mel

Q My mouth feels sore all the time, but looks normal. Should I see my GP?

A Yes – there are many possible causes, including allergies, dry mouth syndrome (sometimes linked to rheumatic diseases or medication, such as drugs for incontinence) and iron or vitamin B12 deficiency. Your GP may change your medication, send you for some blood tests or suggest a dental check if you wear dentures. She can also check for white or red patches, ulcers or lumps, which could be cancerous or pre-cancerous. Thrush sometimes causes soreness without the tell-tale white patches, and occurs in diabetes or after antibiotic or steroid treatment; your GP may suggest trying some miconazole oral gel to see if it helps.

Occasionally, it can be due to burning mouth syndrome, which is often relieved by eating and drinking. The cause isn't known; it may be a form of nerve damage and often improves with tablets that block abnormal nerve signals such as the antidepressant amitriptyline (although this can dry the mouth further). If there is no obvious reason for your sore mouth, she may refer you to a mouth specialist.

In the meantime, keep your mouth well-hydrated with extra drinks, and try soothing glycerine, honey and lemon lozenges from your pharmacy.

TRY THIS Swimming

Aerobic exercise makes your heart pump more efficiently, placing less strain on blood vessels, which helps to reduce high blood pressure. Swimming is one of the most effective exercises. Break your session into 10-minute chunks — one study found people exercising for three 10-minute sessions had lower blood pressure than those exercising solidly for 30 minutes. Stress can also raise blood pressure, and in a survey by swimwear specialists Speedo, 74% of those asked said swimming was a great way to ease tension.

HEALTH ON MY SHELF
Jane Sheehan, reflexologist

What's in your medicine cabinet?
Vitamin C — when colds strike, I take a high dose of 1,000mg. And lavender essential oil. I travel a lot, teaching foot reading, and it helps me to sleep in a new place.

What's good in your fridge?
Innocent smoothies to have with breakfast.

What's your favourite exercise?
Pandiculation! It's all about stretching and yawning. Yawning is great for resetting the nervous system. It's very relaxing.

If you can't sleep, what works?
I read until I feel tired. Or I write down what's on my mind, so I can park it.

What's a special healthy treat?
Pitta bread with hummus and fresh herbs.

Any childhood remedies you still use?
If I had a cold, my mum would always put Vicks VapoRub on the balls of our feet. As a reflexologist, I now know that this area represents the chest, so it makes sense.
To find out more about Jane, visit www. footreading.com

TAKE 5...
Look After Your Eyes

1 HAVE REGULAR EYE TESTS — normally every two years. Many people are entitled to free NHS tests — see www.nhs.uk.

2 SEEK MEDICAL ADVICE promptly if you notice pain and/or vision disturbance.

3 WEAR EYE PROTECTORS when doing DIY, trimming hedges and where corrosive splashes may occur.

4 WEAR WRAPAROUND SUNGLASSES to reduce ultraviolet damage such as cataracts; never look directly at the sun as you may permanently damage your retina.

5 CLEAN contact lenses and storage cases correctly.

10 Monday

11 Tuesday

12 Wednesday

13 Thursday

14 Friday

15 Saturday

16 Sunday

Seashore

Sometimes less really is more, like with this week's easy-knit lightweight sweater — a versatile piece and a quick make, using an interesting random-coloured slub yarn

MEASUREMENTS

To fit sizes 81 (86) (91) (97) (102) (107) cm/32 (34) (36) (38) (40) (42) in.
Actual measurements 92.5 (98) (103.5) (109) (114.5) (120) cm/36½ (38½) (40¾) (43) (45) (47¼) in.
Side seam 38 (39) (39) (40) (40) (41) cm/15 (15¼) (15¼) (15¾) (15¾) (16) in.
Length to back neck 59 (60) (61) (62) (63) (64) cm/23¼ (23½) (24) (24¼) (24¾) (25¼) in.
Sleeve seam 43 (43) (44) (44) (44) (45) cm/17 (17) (17¼) (17¼) (17¼) (17¾) in.

MATERIALS

4 (4) (4) (5) (5) (5) 100g hanks of Colinette Enigma. No. 0 (8mm) and No. 4 (6mm) knitting needles. Yarn costs about £6.60 per 100g hank. We used Morocco (127). For stockists, write to: Colinette Yarns, Banwy Workshops, Llanfair Caereinion, Powys, Wales SY21 0SG (01938 810128; www.colinette. com).

TENSION

11 stitches and 15 rows, to 10 x 10cm, over reverse stocking stitch, using No. 0 (8mm) needles.

ABBREVIATIONS

K, knit; **p,** purl; **st,** stitch; **tog,** together; **dec,** decrease (by taking 2 sts together); **inc,** increase (by working twice in next st); **rss,** reverse stocking st (p on right side and k on wrong side); **nil,** meaning nothing is worked here for this size.

NOTE

Instructions are given for small size. Where they vary, work figures in round brackets for larger sizes. Instructions in square bracket are worked as stated after 2nd bracket.

BACK

With No. 4 (6mm) needles, cast on 87 (92) (97) (102) (107) (112) sts. K 4 rows.
Change to No. 0 (8mm) needles.
Dec row: K2, [k2tog, k2tog, k1] to end — 53 (56) (59) (62) (65) (68) sts.
Beginning with a k row, work in rss until back measures 38 (39) (39) (40) (40) (41) cm/ 15 (15¼) (15¼) (15¾) (15¾) (16) in from cast-on edge. Mark each end of last row for side seams.
Continue in rss until back measures 59 (60) (61) (62) (63) (64) cm/23¼ (23½) (24) (24¼) (24¾) (25¼) in from cast-on edge, ending with a k row.
Shape neck: Next row: P19 (20) (21) (22) (23) (24), turn and work on these sts only for right half neck.
Right half neck: Dec 1 st at neck edge on next 3 rows — 16 (17) (18) (19) (20) (21) sts.
Cast off loosely for shoulder.
Left half neck: With right side facing, slip centre 15 (16) (17) (18) (19) (20) sts on to a st holder, rejoin yarn to remaining sts and p to end — 19 (20) (21) (22) (23) (24) sts.
Dec 1 st at neck edge on next 3 rows — 16 (17) (18) (19) (20) (21) sts.
Cast off loosely for shoulder.

FRONT

With No. 4 (6mm) needles, cast on 87 (92) (97) (102)(107) (112) sts. K 4 rows.
Change to No. 0 (8mm) needles.
Dec row: K2, [k2tog, k2tog, k1] to end — 53 (56) (59) (62) (65) (68) sts.
Beginning with a k row, work in rss until front measures 38 (39) (39) (40) (40) (41) cm/15 (15¼) (15¼) (15¾) (15¾) (16) in from cast-on edge. Mark each end of last row for side seams.
Continue in rss until front measures 54 (55) (56) (57) (58) (59) cm/21¼ (21½) (22) (22¼) (22¾) (23¼) in from cast-on edge, ending with a k row.
Shape neck: Next row: P21 (22) (23) (24) (25) (26), turn and work on these sts only for left half neck.
Left half neck: Dec 1 st at neck edge on next 5 rows — 16 (17) (18) (19) (20) (21) sts.
Continue straight until front measures same as back to shoulder, ending with a k row. Cast off loosely for shoulder.
Right half neck: With right side facing, slip centre 11 (12) (13) (14) (15) (16) sts on to a st holder, rejoin yarn to remaining sts and p to end — 21 (22) (23) (24) (25) (26) sts.
Dec 1 st at neck edge on next 5 rows — 16 (17) (18) (19) (20) (21) sts. Continue straight until front measures same as back to

shoulder, ending with a k row.
Cast off loosely for shoulder.

SLEEVES (BOTH ALIKE)

With No. 4 (6mm) needles, cast on
43 (43) (47) (47) (49) (49) sts.
K 4 rows.
Change to No. 0 (8mm) needles.
Dec row: K2 (2) (1) (1) (2) (2),
[k2tog, k2tog, k1] to last 1 (1) (1) (1)
(2) (2) st(s), p1 (1) (1) (1) (2) (2) — 27
(27) (29) (29) (31) (31) sts.
Beginning with a k row,
rss 3 rows. Continue in rss,
increasing 1 st at each end of next
row and 9 following 4th rows —
47 (47) (49) (49) (51) (51) sts.
Continue straight until sleeve
measures 43 (43) (44) (44)
(44) (45) cm/17 (17) (17¼) (17¼)
(17¼) (17¾) in from cast-on
edge, ending with a k row. Cast
off loosely.

NECKBAND

Join right shoulder seam.
With right side facing and using
No. 4 (6mm) needles, pick up and
k16 sts down left front neck, work
across centre front sts thus: k1 (nil)
(1) (nil) (1) (nil), [inc in next st, k1] 5
(6) (6) (7) (7) (8) times, pick up and
k16 sts up right front neck and 6
sts down right back neck, work
across centre back sts thus: k1 (nil)
(1) (nil) (1) (nil), [inc in next st, k1]
7 (8) (8) (9) (9) (10) times, pick up
and k6 sts up left back neck — 82
(86) (88) (92) (94) (98) sts.
K 2 rows. Cast off kwise.

TO MAKE UP

Join left shoulder and neckband
seam. Sew top edge of sleeves
to row-ends between markers
on back and front. Taking one
stitch into the seam, join side
and sleeve seams.

This scoop-necked sweater with drop shoulders
is knitted entirely in reverse stocking stitch with
tiny garter-stitch edgings. The yarn is cotton-
and-rayon mix, and is hand-wash only.

Llangollen in North Wales

POST — CARD

June Kelsall from Burnham-on-Sea, Somerset, nominates Llangollen, North Wales

'Recently, I visited Llangollen to see the ruins of the 13th-century Valle Crucis Abbey, and I was captivated by the town. I loved Plas Newydd, the home of the famous two Ladies of Llangollen, which has a garden full of sculptured trees and bushes. A few miles down the valley is the magnificent Thomas Telford-designed Pontcysyllte aquaduct, carrying the Llangollen canal over the River Dee.'

Holkham Bay in Norfolk

POST — CARD

Reader Sally Court, from Holme Hale in Norfolk, chooses Holkham Bay

'I would like to nominate Holkham Bay in Norfolk as my favourite place. Not only is there mile after mile of golden sand, but it's also backed by some beautiful woodland. In December, you may have the beach all to yourself, except for the pink-footed geese, who winter in Norfolk. There's no more impressive sight and sound than a cold, grey sky filled with honking wildfowl!'

17 Monday

18 Tuesday

19 Wednesday

20 Thursday

21 Friday

22 Saturday

23 Sunday

Salted Caramel & Chocolate Pots

SERVES *4-5*
CALORIES *873*
FAT *70g*
SATURATED FAT *44g*
SUITABLE FOR FREEZING *No*

FOR THE CARAMEL

* 30g (1oz) unsalted butter
* 100g (3oz) light muscovado sugar
* 150ml carton double cream
* ½ level teaspoon salt flakes, plus extra for decoration

FOR THE CHOCOLATE LAYER

* 300ml carton whipping cream
* 200g bar dark chocolate, melted
* A few drops of vanilla extract
* 4-5 glasses, for serving

1 **To make the caramel:** Melt the butter in a pan and add the sugar and cream. Stir the mixture over a low heat until it dissolves, then increase the heat and simmer the sauce until it thickens slightly to a caramel consistency. Off the heat, leave the caramel to cool for about 10-15 minutes. Stir in the salt flakes. Pour the mixture into the serving glasses and leave to set.

2 **To make the chocolate layer:** Bring the cream to the boil and pour it over the chocolate. Add until the mixture is smooth. Pour the chocolate mixture over the caramel and leave to set. Sprinkle salt flakes over each before serving.

TIP FROM OUR KITCHEN

Whizz the mixture for the chocolate layer with a stick blender to make sure it's smooth.

Aspects Of Love

All that "love" stuff was exhausting, to be honest. It's a relief to be able to get a decent night's sleep and enjoy food again...

Falling in love is overrated, if you ask me. I mean, let's face it, it's not normal — all that not being able to eat or sleep stuff, although I do remember it being quite good for your figure. The not being able to eat bit, anyway. I lost half a stone when I fell in love with Michael. Who wants to live like that? Far better to go on a proper balanced diet, I say.

As for not being able to sleep — well, that bit was awful. I remember one occasion, quite early on, when we'd been to a show. Don't ask me what it was, I haven't a clue. All I do remember is that every time our knees touched accidentally, I felt this amazing warmth steal through me, and when we held hands, well, electricity wasn't the word for it.

He dropped me off home and we kissed good night in my kitchen. The kiss went on for a very long time and the hug went on for longer. I knew he had to go home, he had to get up early in the morning and so did I, but neither of us wanted to part.

"Night, Kath," he said, half a dozen times.

"Night, Michael," I'd whisper back.

He went eventually. He had to, we both knew that. And when he got home, he phoned me up.

"Night, Kath."

"Night, Michael."

Ridiculous — obviously. I mean, how many times do you actually need to say good night?

Then, in the morning, he phoned me up again before he left for work.

"I couldn't sleep last night, Kath."

"I couldn't sleep either."

We might just as well have stayed up doing the kissing and hugging bit.

Now, where was I? Ah yes, love being an overrated pastime for the young and the sentimental. Actually, if I think about it, the very worst thing about falling in love is all that rose-tinted glasses stuff. You know, how everything looks beautiful, even rain, and grey skies, and the Monday morning rush hour. And all those things that usually get right up your nose, like road-works and those answer-phones that say, "Press one for this and two for that," suddenly don't bother you at all.

You decide people like your boss might be human, after all. And you get all forgiving towards other drivers, even the ones who park in the space outside your house and then pretend not to see you as they leg it up to the precinct.

It's great to have a good snap at people who annoy me and take the micky out of slushy love songs

But now, I'm back on the planet again, along with the rest of the sane population, with my feet firmly on solid ground. Thank goodness for that. All that "love" stuff was exhausting, to be honest. It's a relief to be able to get a decent night's sleep. And it's a relief that my stomach isn't doing all that mad butterfly-fluttering and I can actually enjoy my food again.

And it's great to have a good snap at people who annoy me and join in with my mates when they're mercilessly taking the mickey out of slushy love songs and romantic movies.

Good old reality, with all its road-works and ranting bosses, and rain. You can't beat it, can you?

Of course, I have to admit it's nice having someone to share it all with: someone to share grumbles with; someone to cook for who actually clears their plate rather than mooning over it; someone who can walk out of the door without us having to say good night twenty-seven times.

I don't miss Michael. I don't miss him one bit, but that's probably because he's still around. Only now I can see him for what he is: grey hairs, thickening waist-line, and his irritating habit of reading out bits from the Sunday papers when I'm trying to do the crossword.

That's marriage for you. The honeymoon period is well and truly over. Thank goodness. Contentment, familiarity, routine — sitting in a restaurant and being more interested in the menu than gazing into each other's eyes. All those things we used to think would never happen to us, well, actually they're not so bad.

I love them. I love him, too, in a "washing his socks", and "putting up with his rowdy football mates", sort of way. He's great at back rubs, as well — did I mention that?

Not that I've got anything against the odd romantic gesture. Last time we were in the Thirsty Ferret, Michael spelt out *I Love You* with his chips. And he gave me his last one without a blink — said I needed to put a bit of weight on. Not rose-tinted glasses — he'd just forgotten his ordinary ones, or perhaps he needs stronger lenses.

See what I mean about falling in love being overrated? Whereas being IN love; well, that's a different story altogether.

THE END
© Della Galton

24 Monday

25 Tuesday

26 Wednesday

27 Thursday

28 Friday

1 Saturday

2 Sunday

ARROWORD

Moss-like plant / Epoch, era	▼	Nought / — West, film star	▼	Helen of —, mythical beauty	▼	Is in possession of	▼	Measure of distance / Cotton fibre	▼	Shoe without laces (4-2)	▼	Openings in country walls	▼	Ballpoints	▼	Branches
▶				Person who faces facts / Avarice	▶							Flower or part of the eye	▶		
Goods, freight / Hypothesis	▶			▼		More nonsensical	▼							Little waves on water	▼	Flecks
▶						Extensively	▶	— Diamond, US singer / Paradise	▼			Spheres / Quantity of paper	▶			▼	
Adventurous		Mark —, US author	Hires			Showery	▶			Keep trying / Perspiration holes	▶					
▶		▼						Sit (for) / Mouse-like rodent		▶				Animal cages		Tiny parasites
Hand measure	Marry / In favour			Exeter's county / Junky goods	▶			▼		Orchard fruit / Knack				▼		
▶	▼		Range of saxophone	▶						— Earhart, pioneer pilot	▶					
Religious custom / Swindles						Writer of nonsense verse	▶					Long part of a giraffe	▶			
▶		Sorts, kinds	▶							Throws (a pancake)	▶					

SKELETON

Have double the fun with this puzzle — you've got to fill in the answers and the black squares! We've given you the bare bones to start and it will help to know that the black squares in the finished grid form a symmetrical pattern.

ACROSS
1 Brief satirical theatrical scene
3 Unable to be done
10 Further from the centre
11 Cathedral singer
12 Equine transport
13 Inn
15 Itinerary
16 Suppressing
19 Lidded vessel for long slow cooking
21 Muslims' holy city
23 Not perused
25 Lamb and aubergine dish topped with cheese sauce
27 Lay waste
28 Horned African animal
29 All around
30 'Doing' word

DOWN
1 Device for helping the heel into footwear
2 Break continuity
4 Laboratory magnifying device
5 Orchestral instrument which plays the tuning-up note
6 Leafy green vegetable
7 Cleanse
8 Task to be run
9 Gentle wind
14 Saleroom official
17 Smooth-skinned variety of peach
18 Subterranean burial place
20 Tactlessly
21 Unhappiness
22 Rain pool
24 Variety entertainment
26 Declaration to swear the truth in court

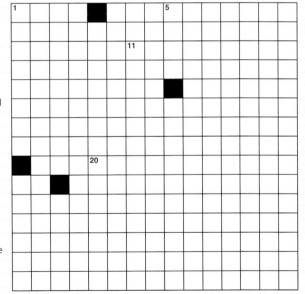

Solutions to this month's puzzle on next month's puzzle

MARCH

St Mary's in Isles of Scilly

POST – CARD

Reader Léonore Ham from Cheddar, Somerset, recommends St Mary's, one of the Isles of Scilly

'You once published a picture of gig racing on the Isles of Scilly, and it prompted so many fond memories. For many years, St Mary's (the largest of the islands) has been my favourite place. The lovely scenery, and the peace and quiet, are truly relaxing. And once you've explored the island, you can catch a boat from the harbour to other parts of this beautiful archipelago.'

Saint-Antonin-Noble-Val in Tarn-et-Garonne, France

POST – CARD

Reader Carol E. Wyer nominates the place where she writes her novels

'The town of Saint-Antonin-Noble-Val in the Tarn-et-Garonne, France, boasts perfectly preserved 11th- and 12th-century buildings, which nestle among formidable gorges, where birds and nature abound. It also found fame in 2001, with the filming of *Charlotte Gray*. I've visited much of France, but the Tarn-et-Garonne, like one of the Greek mythological Sirens, lures me back time after time.'

3 Monday

4 Tuesday

5 Wednesday

6 Thursday

7 Friday

8 Saturday

9 Sunday

Deep-Filled Smoked Haddock & Leek Quiche

SERVES *6*

CALORIES *710*

FAT *56g*

SATURATED FAT *26g*

SUITABLE FOR FREEZING *No*

INGREDIENTS

* 350g (12oz) shortcrust pastry
* 30g (1oz) butter
* 1 tablespoon light olive oil
* 3 leeks, sliced
* 350-400g (12-14oz) smoked haddock, cubed
* 6 medium eggs
* 300ml carton double cream
* Salt and black pepper
* 18cm (7in) round spring-clip tin, buttered
* Baking parchment and baking beans

1 Set the oven to 200°C or Gas Mark 6. Heat a baking sheet. Roll pastry out on a lightly floured surface.

2 Line the tin with the pastry, leaving it just higher than the tin's rim and the edge rough. Use a fork to prick the base. Chill the case, while the oven heats up.

3 Line the pastry case with baking parchment and fill with baking beans. Put the tin on the baking sheet and bake for 15 minutes. Lift out paper with baking beans and bake for 5-10 minutes more.

4 Reduce the oven temperature to 180°C or Gas Mark 4. Melt butter in a pan and add the oil. Cook the leeks over a medium heat for 10-15 minutes, stirring until soft, but don't allow them to colour too much. Remove the pan from heat.

5 Layer up the leeks and raw haddock in the pastry case. Beat eggs with the cream and seasoning and pour into the case.

6 Put the tin back in the oven on the baking sheet and cook for 40-50 minutes, until filling is set.

7 Leave to cool in the tin for a few minutes, then remove from tin and transfer to a wire rack to cool. Serve warm.

Your Good Health

Ask Dr Mel

Q I get terrible leg cramps at night — is it safe to take quinine?

A Night cramps, caused by muscle spasm, can be agonising, and leave muscles feeling sore. They're more common as we get older, possibly because muscle tendons become shorter; they're also linked to pregnancy, exercise, dehydration, infections, liver disease, and neurological conditions. Some medicines trigger them, including diuretics ('water' pills), statins and nicotinic acid (which lower cholesterol levels), nifedipine (used to treat angina and Raynaud's disease) and raloxifene (used to prevent osteoporosis).

Your GP can check for these causes, and may prescribe quinine to take before bed (unless it affects other medicines you may be taking). It's often effective, but can cause nausea, headaches, ringing in the ears, problems with hearing and vision, confusion and abnormal bleeding, so treatment is only recommended for four weeks. Never exceed the dose as this can cause blindness or even death.

Try preventing cramps with stretching exercises during the day and before bed; lean forward against a wall to gently stretch calf muscles; or sit down and pull your toes up towards you. Try walking on your heels, as well as vigorous calf-rubbing, if you still get cramps in the night.

TRY THIS Pilates

The right posture can help you get more energy-giving oxygen into your body. Try this exercise every few hours. Sit tall in a straight-backed chair, with legs uncrossed, stomach muscles pulled in and ribcage lifted, and feel as if you have a string coming from the top of your head down to your tailbone. Breathe down deep into your ribcage and allow it to expand for a full intake of oxygen. Breathe out and repeat three times. Regular Pilates classes will help you to be more posture aware.

HEALTH ON MY SHELF

Joanna Blythman, food writer

What's in your medicine cabinet?
Menthol crystals, for inhaling over steamed water; great for colds. Frankincense hydrating facial mist, which has a glorious aroma that makes me feel fresher.

What's good in your fridge?
Ginger — I have tea with fresh ginger, fennel and fenugreek seeds mid-morning, as it's good for the digestion.

What's your favourite exercise?
I swim 20 lengths as often as possible. It helps me think and gives me energy.

If you can't sleep, what works?
Going downstairs for a herbal tea and sourdough toast. I also listen to Radio 4.

What's a foodie treat?
I adore puddings — tarte tatin, pear and almond tart and crème caramel.

Any childhood remedies you still use?
A hot toddy, made with lemon juice, Manuka honey and malt whisky.
Joanna Blythman is author of What To Eat *(Fourth Estate, £16.99).*

TAKE 5...
Protect Your Voice

1 AVOID STRAINING IT shouting, screaming, coughing, repeated throat-clearing; stay well-hydrated — drink plenty.

2 WAIT UNTIL OTHERS are listening properly, then speak slowly, clearly and at a comfortable volume. Change pitch to emphasise points, rather than speaking more loudly.

3 STAND WELL AND "OPEN" YOUR CHEST by bringing your shoulders back, relaxing and using your breathing to help project your voice.

4 WHEN SINGING, "warm up" first with some gentle exercises such as scales; don't sing if you have a cold.

5 DON'T SMOKE; avoid dusty atmospheres and fumes.

10 Monday

11 Tuesday

12 Wednesday

13 Thursday

14 Friday

15 Saturday

16 Sunday

Have a go at.. Making Soap

Pamper yourself with great-smelling, marbled handmade soap

Our glycerine-rich, natural soap is great fun to make. Using the traditional cold-process method, it takes around two hours (less with a hand blender), but must then be left for 24 hours and "cured" for four to five weeks, before using.

Our recipe, created by Sally Hornsey from Plush Folly, transforms a mixture of oils and shea butter into soap with a "lye" of sodium hydroxide (caustic soda, available from DIY stores) and water.

IMPORTANT SAFETY NOTES

＊Do not use the essential/ fragrance oils undiluted on skin.
＊Sodium hydroxide can cause burns. (There's none left in the soap once it is fully combined with the oils and butter and "cured".) Follow the safety instructions on the container, and wear gloves and goggles.
＊Work in a well-ventilated room and try not to inhale the fumes when you mix the sodium hydroxide into the water.
＊Store the cooling solution out of the reach of children and pets. If you get some on your skin, rinse under cold water for at least 20 minutes. Seek medical advice if concerned about the burn.

To make

1 PREPARING YOUR MOULD
Place the mould liner in the plastic mould and fix in place with pegs or sticky tape. The mould liner is deliberately too big for the mould, as it will also be used to fold over and cover the soap once it has been poured into the mould.

2 PREPARING THE LYE SOLUTION
Wearing gloves and goggles, measure the water into a glass jug and set aside.

In a separate bowl, weigh the sodium hydroxide. Carefully add sodium hydroxide to the water in the jug — never the other way round — carefully stirring until the sodium hydroxide is fully dissolved and has no grainy feel to it when you stir. Set the lye solution aside somewhere safely to allow it to cool.

3 ADDING OILS AND BUTTERS
Place the coconut oil, shea butter and palm oil into a pan large enough to hold at least 1.5 litres of liquid. Place over a low heat and melt the oils and butters very slowly.

Once melted, add the olive oil to the pan. Stir until fully mixed into the other oils. Remove pan from heat.

4 COMBINING LIQUIDS
Paying careful attention to safety as the lye is caustic (wear your gloves and goggles), slowly and carefully pour the lye solution into the pan away from the heat. Start by pouring a very small amount of lye into the oils

---

YOU WILL NEED

All ingredients are measured by weight, not volume. These quantities will make a large slab of soap ready to cut into six generous bars.
＊ *128g coconut oil*
＊ *30g shea butter*
＊ *85g palm oil*
＊ *227g olive oil*
＊ *10g essential oil*

＊ *5g coloured cosmetic clay or natural food colouring*
＊ *70g sodium hydroxide*
＊ *176g water (tap or distilled)*
＊ *Plastic moulds, such as a large margarine or ice-cream tub, or yogurt pots*
＊ *Mould liner, such as cling film*
＊ *Pegs, to hold liner in place*
＊ *Goggles, protective gloves*

and an apron
＊ *Pan — stainless steel but not with a non-stick lining (Don't use an aluminium pang)*
＊ *Spoons*
＊ *Hand-held stick blender, optional*
＊ *Glass or china jug*
＊ *Scales*
＊ *Three towels or a large blanket*

NOTE: *Substituting different oils or butter may cause your soap to be too greasy or too harsh, but you can choose any essential oil for fragrance.*

distribute evenly. The dye will look blue and then turn grey before becoming purple.

8 POURING AND MARBLING

Carefully pour the rest of the mixture (for the uncoloured portion) from the saucepan into the mould, using a spatula to scrape out any residue. Drizzle on the coloured portion and use the end of a spoon to swirl it up and down, as shown above, to create the marbled effect.

Cover the mixture with the overhanging mould liner and put on the lid, then place the mould where it can lie undisturbed for 24 hours at room temperature or warmer. Cover in towels or blankets to insulate it. No peeking! Your soap needs to keep warm or it may become crumbly.

9 UNMOULDING

After 24 hours, you can look at your soap. If it feels "hard", it's ready to remove carefully from the mould. It will still be soft enough for you to cut into bars at this time — but wear gloves as it may still be a bit caustic.

10 CURING

You now need to place your soap somewhere for at least four to five weeks to "cure": it will harden and all traces of caustic will disappear. A dark, cool, dry cupboard is ideal, but anywhere airy will do.

After four to five weeks, your soap will be ready. If you wish, wrap in fabric or cellophane, or greaseproof or handmade paper.

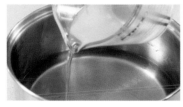

and, if there is no bubbling and hissing, carry on pouring. If there is a reaction, your oils are too hot. Leave them to cool down for ten minutes, then try again.

With the empty jug that contained the lye set safely aside, stir the lye/oil mixture well to ensure that it's thoroughly mixed. Keep stirring carefully but briskly for 2-3 minutes.

5 TRACING

After a few minutes or so, the mixture will turn opaque and start to resemble runny custard — how long this takes depends on the room temperature, the temperature of the oils and the types of oils used.

Keep stirring until a light "trace"

is formed. This is when you can see the mixture start to thicken and if you drizzle a little of the mixture on to the surface, a trail is formed across the surface before it sinks back in. Speed up the tracing process by using a hand-held stick blender, set on a low speed, but be very careful not to splash the mixture out of the pan.

It's perfectly normal for a soap mixture to take minutes, or even hours, to trace, but you don't have to stir constantly: you can stir for a few minutes and then leave the mixture for 15 minutes or so, repeating as necessary.

6 ADDING FRAGRANCE

Once you've reached the trace stage, which is when the mixture has thickened like custard and leaves a trail on the surface when drizzled, add the essential oil and continue to mix until thoroughly combined.

7 ADDING COLOUR

Pour a little mixture into a jug, and add the clay, or food colouring, to it. Stir well to

Experience

They've put me in Men's Clothing in the most un-cool store in town. Nobody my age would be seen dead anywhere near it

I can hear her footsteps coming. "Tom? Tom? Come on, my lad, time to shake a leg. Big day today." I let out a sound, half groan, half moan, which makes the footsteps go away. Mothers! When and where do they learn these stupid words? "Lad", for instance. OK, I suppose I'm not quite a man. But I'm fifteen now and I shave once a week and I'm taller than she is.

She's right about one thing. It is a big day today — big pain, big headache. My first day of work experience. Some of the kids in my class have got it made. Mick, for instance, is going to work in his dad's garage. The boffins and the super-keen have fixed up some brilliant placements. Mel is going to work backstage in a West End theatre, Danny's going to a fire station, Speccy Bates is working as a reporter on the local paper.

I like to play it cool. That's what I'm known for at school. So, to keep up my image, I showed no interest whatsoever in this work experience lark, in spite of endless nagging from school and Mum. And because I didn't fix anything up myself, I've been landed with a week at the poshest, most un-cool department store in town. Camel Brothers, it's called. Nobody my age would be seen dead anywhere near it. And not only do I have to work there for a week, I have to wear a kind of uniform. Including a tie with camels dotted all over it. It's criminal.

By nine am, I'm in the manager's office and he dishes out a gross yellow jacket, the camel tie and a major pep-talk. And to make matters fifty zillion times worse, Becky Stilling is there in the office with me. She's in my class and she actually volunteered to work here. I'm keen on Becky, only I haven't let her know it yet. She gives me a bit of a wink and a smile as we stand and listen to our instructions. But I'm not sure if she's being friendly or taking the micky out of my jacket and tie, so I don't smile back.

Anyway, Becky sashays off to the make-up and perfume department on the ground floor and I am led up to the fifth floor — Men's Clothing. I have to shadow this salesman called Julian. He's old, old, old — in his thirties. I follow him about, listen to his "Can I help you, Sir?", "Can I help you, Madam?" until my ears are about to drop off. I learn one important thing about men's clothing. It's women that buy it. Women like my mum.

> *Every time I think of Becky, my face burns bright red. I've blown it with her*

By lunch-time, my feet are killing me. But they've given me a food voucher and, as I'm in the queue deciding what to buy, I spot Becky having her lunch in the corner. She's sitting with two other girls, but there's a vacant seat nearby. I choose the coolest items I can spot on the menu — a large latte and a ham and cheese pannini. I would rather have a beefburger and chips, but I want to impress Becky.

As I make my way towards her, she looks up, sees me and waves. I sort of wiggle a finger at her, very casually, and concentrate on walking without dropping my tray.

But as I get nearer, I see that all three girls have burst into shrieks of laughter — and Becky is pointing towards me and laughing the most. Totally cracking up. Too late, I spot that I have walked across the restaurant with my camel tie drooping down into my large latte. I sit down, quick as I can, and attempt to sort myself out. But the tie is soaked and coffee splurges over my clean white shirt and splashes on to my yellow jacket. This is the most un-cool moment of my entire life. I leave my lunch and make a dash for the exit.

Julian is surprisingly helpful over my stained clothes. Somehow, I get through the long afternoon. But every time I think of Becky, my face burns bright red. I've blown it with her. She'll never take me seriously now.

When I get home, I dash straight up to my room and put on my music. Within minutes, I hear Mum bashing on my door. She wants to know how my day went, and gradually I find myself telling her. She has her ways. When I get to the tie bit, she laughs too. But she sees my face and stops — and then I tell her about Becky.

She sits and stares at me and says nothing for ages. I wait.

"You know what we girls like best in a man?" she says at last. "It's not rippling muscles or any of that. We like a man who can make us laugh. Think about it."

Mothers! What do they know? Anyhow, after a while I get out my mobile and text Becky. I've had her number for ages.

"Did u like my awesome tie trick?" I write. *"I did it 4 u. More 2morrow."*

She texts me back, straight away.

"Can't wait," she says. *"C u, love Becky xx"*

I lie back on my bed, arms behind my head. Work experience? Bring it on.

THE END

© Patricia Findel-Hawkins

17 Monday

18 Tuesday

19 Wednesday

20 Thursday

21 Friday

22 Saturday

23 Sunday

Too Good To Eat

Which is just as well, as these colourful cupcakes are for you to knit, not nibble on!

MEASUREMENTS
Each cupcake measures 8cm/3in in diameter and 7cm/2¾in high, excluding decorations.

MATERIALS
1 x 50g ball of Rico Essential Cotton DK in each of White (80), Yellow (63), Dusky Pink (19), Rose (01), Fuchsia (14), Mint (64), Grass (66) and Pistachio (86). Pair of 2¼mm (No. 13), 2¾mm (No. 12) and 3mm (No. 11) knitting needles; small amount of washable toy stuffing. Yarn costs approximately £2.50 per 50g ball. For yarn stockists, call 020 3024 9009. The yarn can be purchased from Crafty Yarn (0118 943 1144; www.crafty-yarn.co.uk), or Black Sheep (01925 764231; www. blacksheepwools.co.uk) or Multi Ply (01723 364191; www.multiplywools. co.uk).

TENSION
26 stitches and 34 rows, to 10 x 10cm, over stocking stitch, using 3mm needles.

ABBREVIATIONS
K, knit; **p,** purl; **st,** stitch; **tog,** together; **inc,** increase (by working twice in same st); **dec,** decrease (by taking 2 sts tog); **ss,** stocking st (k on right side and p on wrong side); **sl,** slip.

NOTE
Yarn amounts are based on average requirements and are therefore approximate. Instructions in square brackets are worked as stated after 2nd bracket.

CUPCAKES

Base: With 2¼mm needles and White, cast on 12 sts for base. P 1 row.
1st inc row: [Inc kwise in next st] to end — 24 sts. P 1 row.
2nd inc row: [Inc, k1] to end — 36 sts. P 1 row.
3rd inc row: [Inc, k2] to end — 48 sts. P 1 row.

P 1 row for fold line.
Side: Work 6 rows in k1, p1 rib.
Change to 2¾mm needles.
Rib another 6 rows.
Change to 3mm needles.
Rib another 6 rows. K 1 row.
Icing: Change to Dusky Pink.
Beginning with a k row, ss 2 rows.
1st dec row: [K4, k2tog] to end
— 40 sts.
Next row: P3, [k8, p5] twice, k8,
p3. K 1 row and p 1 row.
2nd dec row: [K3, k2tog] to end
— 32 sts. P 1 row.
Next row: P2, [k4, p4] 3 times, k4,
p2. P 1 row.
3rd dec row: [K2, k2tog] to end
— 24 sts. P 1 row.
4th dec row: [K1, k2tog] to end
— 16 sts.
Next row: [K3, p4] twice, k2.
Next row: [K2tog] to end — 8 sts.
P 1 row.
Break off yarn, leaving a long end.
Thread end through remaining
sts, pull up and fasten off.
Gather cast on-edge, pull up
tightly and secure. Join row-ends,
leaving an opening. Stuff firmly
and close opening.
Using first colour instead of
White and second colour instead
of Dusky Pink, make one more
cake in each of following colour
combinations: Fuchsia and Rose,
Mint and Grass, Pistachio and
Fuchsia, Dusky Pink and Fuchsia,
Yellow and Grass, Fuchsia and
Yellow, Grass and Pistachio.

Daffodils

Petals: With 2¼mm needles and
Yellow, cast on 10 sts.
1st row: Sl1, k9. **2nd row:** P7.
3rd row: K5. **4th row:** P4.
5th row: K6. **6th row:** P8, p2tog.
7th row:
Cast off
7, place
st used in
casting
off back
on to left
needle

and cast on 8 sts — 10 sts.
Repeat last 7 rows, 4 times more,
then work 1st to 6th rows again.
Cast off.
Centre: With 2¼mm needles,
and yellow, cast on 12 sts.
Beginning with a k row, ss
6 rows.
Inc row: K1, inc, [k3, inc] twice,
k2 — 15 sts. P 1 row. Cast off in
k1, p1 rib.
Beginning at straight edge
of petals, join first 2 stitches
of cast-on and cast-off edges
together. Gather cast-on edge
of centre, pull up and secure,
then join row-ends together.
Place gathered end of centre in
the middle of petals and sew in
position. Sew flower to top of cake.
Make one more flower in same
way and 2 more using White
instead of Yellow for petals.

Mini Eggs

With 2¼mm needles and White,
cast on 5 sts for base.
1st inc row: [Inc kwise in next st]
to end — 10 sts. P 1 row.
2nd inc row: [Inc, k1] to end —
15 sts. Ss 5 rows.
1st dec row: [K2, k2tog] 3 times,
k3 — 12 sts. P 1 row.
2nd dec row: [K1, k2tog] to end
— 8 sts. P 1 row.
3rd dec row: [K2tog] to end —
4 sts.
Break off yarn, leaving a long end.
Thread end through remaining
sts, pull up and fasten off.
Gather cast-on edge, then join
row-ends together, leaving an
opening.
Stuff
firmly
and close
opening.
Make
2 more
eggs in

White, 2 eggs in each of Dusky
Pink and Fuchsia and 1 egg in
each of Yellow, Rose, Mint, Grass
and Pistachio.
Arrange eggs of various colours
in 4 groups of 3 eggs each.
Thread length of yarn lengthways
through centre of 3 eggs and join
into a triangle. Place this triangle
on top of cake and sew
in position.

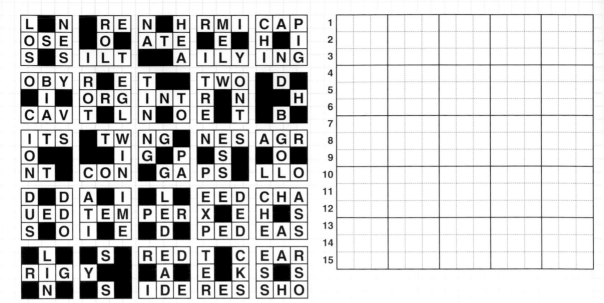

PIECEWORD

Using the across clues to help you, transfer the jigsaw pieces into the blank grid to form a crossword that is symmetrical from top to bottom and left to right.

ACROSS

1 Laterally in pairs (3 words) • State the main points again
3 Having a surface which curves inwards • Sloping
5 Wild drunken party • Mild (climate)
7 Prince ___, panto character • Shared the same view
9 Without difficulty • Ran like a horse
11 Aroused the curiosity of • Garden watering tube
13 Sincere and serious • List of names at the end of a film
15 Places to buy things • Person living in a place

BRICKWORK

Enter the answers to the clues in the bricks. Every word is an anagram of its neighbours, plus or minus a letter.

1 First letter of the alphabet (1)
2 Yes, indeed (2)
3 Beam of light (3)
4 Twelve-month period (4)
5 Ahead of time (5)
6 Action ___, part of a game shown again (6)
7 Herb often used as a garnish (7)
8 Render immobile (8)

Solutions to this month's puzzle on next month's puzzle

24 Monday

25 Tuesday

26 Wednesday

27 Thursday

28 Friday

29 Saturday

30 Sunday

APRIL

31 Monday

1 Tuesday

2 Wednesday

3 Thursday

4 Friday

5 Saturday

6 Sunday

Twinkle Toes

This little piggy went to market, this little piggy stayed at home...and this little piggy was cosy in its pretty bootees

MATERIALS

Blue sandals: 1 x 50g ball of Debbie Bliss Cashmerino in Pale Blue (202). 2 buttons.

Cream shoes: 1 x 50g ball of Debbie Bliss Cashmerino in Ecru (101). 2 buttons.

Bootees: 1 x 50g ball of Debbie Bliss Cashmerino in Teal (203).

For all items: A pair of 3mm (No. 11) knitting needles. Yarn costs about £4.75 per 50g ball. For yarn stockists, write to: Designer Yarns Ltd, Unit 8-10 Newbridge Industrial Estate, Pitt Street, Keighley, West Yorkshire BD21 4PQ (01535 664222).

TENSION

28 stitches and 37 rows, to 10 x 10cm, over stocking stitch, using 3mm needles.

28 stitches and 50 rows, to 10 x 10cm, over garter stitch (every row k), using 3mm needles.

ABBREVIATIONS

K, knit; **p,** purl; **st,** stitch; **tog,** together; **sl,** slip; **ss,** stocking st (k on right side and p on wrong side); **yf,** yarn forward to make a st; **k1b,** k1 through back of st; **skpo,** sl1, k1, pass sl st over.

NOTE

Yarn amounts are based on average requirements and are therefore approximate. Instructions in square brackets are worked as stated after 2nd bracket.

Blue sandals

RIGHT SANDAL

With 3mm needles, cast on 36 sts for centre of sole. K 1 row.

1st row (right side): K1, yf, k16, yf, [k1, yf] twice, k16, yf, k1.

2nd and every following alternate rows: K to end, working k1b in each yf of previous row.

3rd row: K2, yf, k16, yf, k2, yf, k3, yf, k16, yf, k2.

5th row: K3, yf, k16, yf, [k4, yf] twice, k16, yf, k3.

7th row: K4, yf, k16, yf, k5, yf, k6, yf, k16, yf, k4.

9th row: K5, yf, k16, yf, [k7, yf] twice, k16, yf, k5.

11th row: K22, yf, k8, yf, k9, yf, k22 — 64 sts.

12th row: As 2nd row.

Beginning with a k row, ss 7 rows.

Next row: [P next st tog with corresponding st 7 rows below st on needle] to end.

Beginning with a k row, ss 8 rows.

Shape instep: 1st row: K36, skpo, turn.

2nd row: Sl1, p8, p2tog, turn.

3rd row: Sl1, k8, skpo, turn.

4th to 18th rows: Repeat 2nd and 3rd rows, 7 times more, then work 2nd row again.

19th rows: Sl1, k to end.

20th row: K17, k2tog, p8, skpo, k17 — 44 sts.

Divide for front strap: Next row: K24, turn.

Next row: P4, turn.

Next row: K4, turn.

Beginning with a p row, ss 24 rows. Cast off.

With right side facing, begin at base of front strap and using right-hand needle holding 20 sts, pick up and k15 sts along row-ends of one side of front strap — 35 sts.

Cast off first 26 sts kwise, k to end — 9 sts. Leave these 9 sts on a safety pin.

With right side facing, begin at cast-off edge of front strap, pick up and k15 sts along row-ends of other side of front strap, then k remaining 20 sts — 35 sts.

K9 and leave on a safety pin, then cast off remaining 26 sts.

Ankle strap: Join sole and heel seam. With right side facing, k across 9 sts on safety pins — 18 sts. **

Next row: Cast on 22 sts, k across these sts, k to end, turn and cast on 4 sts — 44 sts.

Buttonhole row: K to last 3 sts, yf, k2tog, k1.

K 1 row. Cast off kwise.

Fold end of front strap over ankle strap and catch down cast-off edge on the inside. Sew on button.

LEFT SANDAL

Work as given for right sandal to **.

Next row: Cast on 4 sts, k across these 4 sts, k to end, turn and cast on 22 sts — 44 sts.

Buttonhole row: K1, skpo, yf, k to end.

K 1 rows. Cast off kwise.

Fold end of front strap over ankle strap and catch down cast-off edge on the inside. Sew on button.

Booties

BOTH FEET

With 3mm needles, cast on 18 sts for first half cuff.

K 12 rows.

Break off yarn and leave these sts on a st holder.

With 3mm needles, cast on 18 sts for second half cuff. K 12 rows, but do not break off yarn.

From left to right:
**Blue sandals,
cream shoes,
bootees**

twice, k16, yf, k5.
11th row: K22, yf, k8, yf, k9, yf, k22 — 64 sts.
12th row: As 2nd row. K 12 rows.
Shape instep: 1st row: K36, skpo, turn.
2nd row: Sl1, p8, p2tog, turn.
3rd row: Sl1, k8, skpo, turn.
4th to 14th rows: Repeat 2nd and 3rd rows, 5 times more, then work 2nd row again.
15th row: Sl1, k to end.
16th row: k19, k2tog, p8, skpo, k19 — 48 sts.
Dividing row: K9 and leave these sts on a safety pin, work picot thus: Cast off 1 st, [sl st on right-hand needle back on to left-hand needle, cast on 2 sts, then cast off 4 sts] 14 times, sl st from right-hand needle back on to left-hand needle, cast on 2 sts, then cast off 3 sts, k to end, leaving remaining 9 sts on a safety pin.
Ankle strap: Join sole and heel seam. With wrong side facing, rejoin yarn to remaining 18 sts and k to end. **
Next row: Cast on 4 sts, k across these 4 sts, k to end, turn and cast on 22 sts — 44 sts. K 1 row.
Buttonhole row: K to last 3 sts, yf, k2tog, k1. K 1 row. Cast off kwise. Sew on button.

LEFT SHOE

Work as given for right shoe to **.
Next row: Cast on 22 sts, k across these 22 sts, k to end, turn and cast on 4 sts — 44 sts.
K 1 row.
Buttonhole row: K1, skpo, yf, k to end. K 1 row. Cast off kwise. Sew on button.

Cream shoes

RIGHT SHOE

With 3mm needles, cast on 36 sts for centre of sole. K 1 row.
1st row (right side): K1, yf, k16, yf, [k1, yf] twice, k16, yf, k1.
2nd and every following alternate rows: K to end, working k1b in each yf of previous row.
3rd row: K2, yf, k16, yf, k2, yf, k3, yf, k16, yf, k2.
5th row: K3, yf, k16, yf, [k4, yf] twice, k16, yf, k3.
7th row: K4, yf, k16, yf, k5, yf, k6, yf, k16, yf, k4.
9th row: K5, yf, k16, yf, [k7, yf]

Joining row: [K1, p1] 9 times across sts of second half cuff, then [k1, p1] 9 times across sts of first half — 36 sts.
Rib row: [K1, p1] to end.
Repeat the last row, 6 times more.
Shape instep: Next row (right side): K23, turn.
Next row: K10, turn.
K 24 rows across 10 sts at centre.
Next row: K1, skpo, k4, k2tog, k1 — 8 sts.
K 1 row. Break off yarn and leave sts.

With right side facing, rejoin yarn to base of instep, with right-hand needle holding 13 sts, pick up and k13 sts evenly along side of instep, k8 sts at centre, pick up and k13 sts evenly along other side of instep, then k remaining 13 sts — 60 sts.
K 13 rows.
Beginning with a k row, ss 7 rows.
Next row: [P next st tog with corresponding st 7 rows below st on needle] to end. Break off yarn.
Shape sole: With right side facing, sl first 25 sts on to right-hand needle, rejoin yarn and k10 sts, turn.
Next row: K9, k2tog, turn.
Repeat last row, 39 times more — 20 sts. Cast off.
Join centre back seam.
With back seam at centre of cast-off edge of sole, join heel seam.

Your Good Health

Ask Dr Mel

Q Which is better for weight loss — a high-protein breakfast, a high-fat one or a high-carb one? I'm confused as there is so much contradictory advice.

A Over a quarter of us are now obese, with increased health risks, so many of us are looking for simple ways to lose weight, apart from the traditional "eat less, move more".

Current UK dietary guidelines recommend that starchy (carbohydrate) foods such as potatoes, bread and pasta should make up around a third of our daily food intake (not necessarily every meal). Recent Swedish research has suggested that women who eat low-carbohydrate, high-protein diets may be more prone to cardiovascular disease. But this is open to debate, as their diets were only analysed once at the start of the 15-year study, and by the women themselves, not dietary experts.

It's also recommended that we limit our fat intake and opt for unsaturated fats in oily fish, nuts and avocados where possible, although US researchers say low-fat diets may lead to yo-yo weight gain by altering how many calories we need. I do think it's important to eat enough breakfast, however, and an egg or portion of mackerel, plus porridge or wholewheat cereals/toast should help to keep you fuller for longer, and stop you snacking before lunch.

TRY THIS | Walking Better

Putting a little more effort into your exercise every day will make a real difference. To strengthen your legs, go at a brisk pace and include hill training — walk or jog uphill at a steady pace for 30 yards and then back down. Repeat up to five times. To ring the changes, walk/jog up backwards. A good long walk once a week will give your workout a good balance. A pedometer or sports watch makes it easier to set goals and log your distance and time.

HEALTH ON MY SHELF
Trisha Buller, trichologist

What's in your medicine cabinet?
Skin Marvel: it's great for my urticaria; and Ambrotose capsules for immune support.

What's good in your fridge?
Celery, which is a diuretic. With fat-free hummus, it resolves any hunger pangs.

What's your favourite exercise?
Having spent years road running and damaging my knees, I now see a personal trainer one to three times a week.

If you can't sleep, what works?
I have my iPad next to my bed and type what's on my mind. This clears my thought patterns and helps me to get back to sleep.

What's a special healthy treat?
Baked sea bass at my favourite restaurant.

What makes you happy?
Time with my grandchildren gives me the warmest feeling possible.

Any childhood remedies you still use?
Karvol. My mum used to put it into a bowl and hang a towel over my head. You inhale the fumes to clear blocked sinuses.

TAKE 6...
Avoid A Fragility Fracture

1 DON'T SMOKE, and drink alcohol only in moderation.

2 EAT AT LEAST 700mg calcium daily (equivalent to a pint of milk).

3 TAKE A DAILY 10mcg vitamin D supplement if you're pregnant, breastfeeding, over 65, have dark skin or are housebound.

4 DO WEIGHT-BEARING EXERCISE (eg, walking) to strengthen bones.

5 DO MUSCLE-STRENGTHENING exercises (eg, free weight-lifting) to improve your balance.

6 TAKE THE National Osteoporosis Society's online test to check your bone health at www.nos.org.uk/risk.

7 Monday

8 Tuesday

9 Wednesday

10 Thursday

11 Friday

12 Saturday

13 Sunday

Easter Passion Cake

SERVES 16
CALORIES 410
FAT 31g
SATURATED FAT 12g
SUITABLE FOR FREEZING Yes

INGREDIENTS

* 300g (10oz) golden caster sugar
* 3 medium eggs
* 300ml (½ pint) sunflower oil
* 1 teaspoon vanilla extract
* 300g (10oz) self-raising flour, sieved
* 2 teaspoons ground cinnamon
* 60g (2oz) desiccated coconut
* 150g (5oz) carrot, peeled and grated
* 225g can pineapple in juice, drained and crushed in a blender

FILLING AND DECORATION

* 500g carton mascarpone cheese
* 1 tablespoon vanilla extract
* 60g (2oz) caster sugar
* 8 tablespoons lemon curd
* Good handful of mini sugared eggs
* 2 x 20cm (8in) round cake tins, lined with baking parchment

1 Set the oven to 190°C or Gas Mark 5. Put the sugar, eggs, sunflower oil and vanilla into a bowl and whisk with an electric mixer for a few minutes, until pale and well combined.

2 Sieve in the flour and cinnamon. Add the coconut, carrot and pineapple. Gently fold everything together. Divide mixture between the tins. Bake for 30 minutes, until well-risen, golden and shrinking away from the sides of the tin. Turn out on to a wire rack to cool.

3 **To make the filling:** Put the mascarpone, vanilla and sugar in a bowl and mix together until smooth.

4 Slice each cake in half, horizontally. Put the base of 1 cake on to a cake stand or serving plate, spread with 4 tablespoons lemon curd. Top with another cake and spread with half the flavoured mascarpone. Repeat with the other 2 layers of cake and arrange the sugared eggs on top.

TIP FROM OUR KITCHEN

The sugared Easter eggs tend to soften and the colours run, so pop them on the cake just before serving.

Bickleigh in Devon

POST – CARD

Reader Ivy Surtees, from West Moors in Dorset, chooses the village of Bickleigh in Devon

'Bickleigh, to the north of Exeter in East Devon, and sitting on the River Exe, is a little piece of heaven. Visiting there is like stepping back in time as the village is so peaceful with its lovely thatched cottages. Walking by the Exe, admiring the reflections while you listen to the birds sing, is absolutely wonderful, and it's without doubt my very favourite place!'

Marsden Bay in County Durham

POST – CARD

Reader Jackie Patrick, from Hayling Island, Hampshire, nominates Marsden Bay in County Durham

'I love the rugged coastline of Marsden Bay, near South Shields, with its impressive rock formations and views to Tynemouth Priory and Souter Lighthouse. Defying the elements, magnificent solitary stacks stand 100-feet high, surrounded by the sea. Associated in the past with smugglers and shipwrecks, it is home to cormorants, gulls, fulmars and kittiwakes.'

14 Monday

15 Tuesday

16 Wednesday

17 Thursday

18 Friday GOOD FRIDAY

19 Saturday

20 Sunday

Centre Of Attention

These simple makes and styling ideas will brighten up your table

Fabric-Covered Easter Eggs

TIP
If you're short on time, just decorate a few eggs and mix them in with some undecorated ones — you'll still have a lovely display.

Fortuna dessert bowl, £65, Dartington Crystal (01805 626221; www.dartington. co.uk). Soul Blossoms Fuchsia Tree fabric by Amy Butler, £10.70 per metre; Playnation tumbler in blue and pink, £4 each, all John Lewis (0845 604 9049; www.johnlewis.com)

yet different looks, but you could use a variety of fabrics to adorn your eggs.

3 Mix up an equal measure of PVA glue and water in a small, shallow bowl and stir well. Take an egg and rest it on an upturned bottle lid to raise it off your worktop. Submerge your first piece of cut fabric into the glue, then wipe most of it off on the side of the bowl so that it's coated but not dripping. Lay it in place on the egg then, using a paintbrush or your fingers, smooth it into place. Once all the corners are smoothed down, dampen the tip of a cotton-wool bud and wipe off any excess glue. Leave to dry thoroughly — if any edges start to lift, simply add a little more glue.

Use découpage to decorate eggs and put them in a bowl to create a pretty centrepiece.

YOU WILL NEED
✳ *Six white duck eggs* ✳ *Large needle or pin* ✳ *Lightweight cotton fabric with a floral pattern* ✳ *PVA glue* ✳ *Small paintbrush* ✳ *Fabric scissors* ✳ *Cotton-wool buds*

1 Blow out your eggs by making a hole in the top and bottom with the large needle or pin, making sure that you pierce through the yolk (if you find blowing the egg too tricky, try using a turkey baster). Once all the egg is out, rinse through and leave to dry.

2 Cut out fabric motifs ready to start your découpage. For any larger pieces, make small incisions every 1cm around their edge to allow the motif to fit round the curves of the egg. We chose a fabric that features several different small floral designs to give us a number of coordinating

Egg Cup Candles

TIP
Display eggs in small terracotta plant pots. We painted ours in white emulsion and added the left-over food dye to colour them.

Egg-Filled Vases

Style a floral display that looks good enough to eat.

1 Fit a clear glass jar, bowl or container filled with water inside each larger vase, to place your flowers in. For any small or thin vases, where you'll only use a few sprigs, add a water pocket around each stem or arrangement instead by creating a cellophane pouch filled with water surrounding the end of the stalk(s), fixed on with gaffer tape.

2 For larger vases, fill the void between the inner container and vase with white paper shred until container is almost covered, then add chocolate eggs around the top. Once done, arrange your flowers. For smaller arrangements, first add your flowers with their water pockets attached, and then add your chocolate eggs, either half or completely filling each vase.

TIP
This project could easily be adapted by using a run of smaller vases to create a decorative feature along a windowsill or fireplace.

Flower bouquet vase (22cm high), £32; Flower sprig vase (11cm high), £12; Pablo vase (20cm high), £10, all LSA (www.lsa-international.com). White Kraft paper shred, £3.75 for 200g, Jaffa Imports (01502 511399; www.cheapwicker baskets. co.uk). Chicky Choccy Speckled Mini Eggs, £1.19 per bag, M&S (0845 302 1234; www. marksandspencer.com). Crazy Daisy side plate, £48 for four, Portmeirion (01782 744721; www.portmeirion.co.uk). Napkin, £16 for four, Debenhams (0844 561 6161; www.debenhams.com)

Set the scene with these twinkly tea-lights.

1 Hard-boil your eggs. When cool, break off the top at two-thirds up and scrape out the egg. Clean the remaining shell inside and out, breaking off loose bits to leave a jagged edge.

2 Dye your eggshell. To tint the whole egg leaving a white rim, add half a teaspoon of white wine vinegar and food colouring in equal measures into the jam jar and fill with hot water. Fill your eggshell about three-quarters full with water and place it in the jar, allowing it to bob. Adjusting the amount of water will make it sit higher or lower, giving you a thicker or thinner white band at the top. To tint a band of colour at the top of the egg, use the same ratio of vinegar and dye in a jam-jar lid, adding a small amount of hot water, and place your egg upside down in the mix. Keep an eye on the eggs. Remove

when you're happy with the colour; the longer you leave them, the stronger the colour will be.

3 Take a tea-light, remove it from its metal casing and pull out the wick from the bottom. Place tea-light in the ladle and hold over the edge of a gas hob, making sure your hand isn't too close to the flame. Once the wax has melted, let it cool for a minute before pouring it into your eggs, Check that they're well supported and upright (try putting them back in their egg box). When the wax begins to thicken, after about ten minutes, replace the wick and leave to fully set before use.

PME food colouring, from a selection at Blue Ribbons (020 8941 1591; www.blueribbons.co.uk). Mini flower pots (48mm high), £3.75 for ten, Rainbow Florist Supplies (0800 212869; www.rainbowflorist supplies.co.uk). Green twisted yarn table runner by Rocha, John Rocha, £20, Debenhams (details as above)

Finding Mr Right

It was all Jane's idea — and she would be smug beyond belief now the search was over

Tammy watched him through the glass panel in the door. Even from this distance, she could tell he was a bit of a hunk. Sharp suit. Short, neat hair. Strong jaw. Square shoulders.

He pulled back a cuff and glanced at his watch. Did that mean he was a stickler for punctuality? Or did it mean he was having second thoughts and was wondering how long he could leave it, before getting up and walking out?

"I wouldn't keep that waiting," Jane said, peering over her shoulder. "In fact, if you don't hurry up, I might just have him for myself."

Tammy couldn't take her eyes off him. "He's certainly the best-looking one yet," she admitted. "Much better than that last one."

She walked over to the Adonis seated by the yucca tree. He smiled

"Much, much better," Jane agreed. "Oh, that hair! Did you ask him if he had shares in a gel factory?"

"Looks aren't everything though," Tammy said.

"They're a start," Jane muttered.

"I mean, he could be awful. A thicko. Or a male chauvinist pig. Or both."

"He doesn't look like either." Jane sighed longingly. "Or he could be Mr Right."

"Well, here goes then," Tammy said, smoothing her skirt. "Wish me luck."

"Just remember," Jane whispered as Tammy pushed the door open, "if he turns out to be as wonderful as he looks, this was all my idea."

Tammy walked over to the Adonis seated by the yucca tree. He smiled as she approached and rose from his seat to shake her hand politely.

"Tammy Chapman, I presume," he said, his voice sexy and a little gravelly.

"Hello," she said, thinking how blue his eyes were. "You must be Jason Parker."

"That's me." He smiled again.

There was a moment of awkwardness as both made a move to sit, neither wanting to be first, neither wanting to be last. Tammy suppressed a nervous giggle.

"So...nice weather we're having."

They both looked to the window — where the wind and rain were lashing against the pane. "I quite like storms too," he said, a playful smile on his lips. "They're always... oddly romantic."

Oh, heck! Tammy cringed inside. It was always the same. Brain stalled on the runway.

This was all Jane's fault. It had been her idea to put her requirements on the website.

"You need someone," Jane had said, one Friday evening after a hard week at the office.

"I do just fine on my own," Tammy had protested.

"I've seen you — chained to your desk, working all the time. When was the last time you walked hand-in-hand through the park? When was the last time you—"

"All right, all right!" Tammy had held her hands up. She knew what her life was like. She didn't need her nose rubbing in it.

Jane had composed the ad for her.

"You don't want any old duffer answering this," Jane had said. "You want to find Mr Right. It's all in the wording. Trust me."

Tammy had trusted her, posted the ad and waited impatiently for the replies to flood in. There had been no flood, only a trickle. The first two had sounded fine in their e-mails but, in the flesh, they had been a different matter altogether. The first had been desperate, virtually on his hands and knees for her to accept him.

And then the man with the ultra-gelled hair had turned up.

But now, Tammy was beginning to think that maybe Jane's idea hadn't been such a bad one after all.

"What made you reply to my advertisement?" Tammy asked, after they had exchanged small talk for a couple of minutes.

Jason Parker looked deep into her eyes. "It appealed to me," he said. "I read it and I thought to myself, 'I am the man you are looking for'."

While Jason talked, Tammy knew he was exactly the man she was looking for. After only the third attempt, she had found her Mr Right.

Who would have thought that Jane's idea would have worked so well? Jane would be smug beyond belief once she told her the search was over.

Tammy felt a warm glow inside as she chatted with Jason Parker. She thought of evenings out, holding hands in the park, romantic nights of passion. These were the things that were missing from her life. For so long, she had simply worked.

And so, as their first meeting came to an end, Tammy rose to her feet and shook Jason Parker's hand. She knew he was the man for her.

"I'll be in touch," she told him. "Although I will say you stand a very good chance of getting the job."

Jason Parker grinned happily and Tammy knew her husband would be pleased she had finally got an assistant to ease her workload. It was about time she put her marriage before her job.

THE END
© Steve Beresford

21 Monday EASTER MONDAY

22 Tuesday

23 Wednesday

24 Thursday

25 Friday

26 Saturday

27 Sunday

CRYPTIC

ACROSS

1 Team gave deep breath, audibly (4)
3 Garbled rap session slurs (10)
10 Part of church where you'll hear 'I will' briefly (5)
11 Something said possibly cuter and neat (9)
12 Two instruments for nautical dance (8)
13 Would Frank cede Belgium over a bit of spruce? (6)
15 Blyton creation, out of place in New York (5)
16 Hold 'Sir' out for page as noble title (8)
19 People looking hard round back of restaurant for appetisers (8)
21 Boss almost makes silly mistake (5)
23 Tear-jerkers in soon for reorganisation (6)
25 Dicky uses same rubber (8)
27 When exaggerated they become mountains (9)
28 Wise Premium Bond selector (5)
29 Salt as a final recourse? (4,6)
30 Support the others (4)

DOWN

1 Harshly critical about careless chats over gin sling (8)
2 With token, tried to shift black mark (9)
4 Garden killer needs two bullets (4,6)
5 Warms up missing starter and devours (4)
6 Son very mistakenly interrupted American inspections (7)
7 Oz snow leopard? (5)
8 Arab leader heard to tremble (6)
9 Jack to work steadily and intensely (6)

14 Press tears off to find unwelcome visitor (10)
17 Clout funnel perhaps, during chilliness (9)
18 Respectful always in housing payment (8)
20 Person rearing cattle dashed and caught her (7)
21 Turn on charm, almost, and that's the truth (6)
22 It's customary to be a bit malign or malicious (6)
24 Lies about southern pieces of land (5)
26 A girl is heard. Oh dear! (4)

ADD A LETTER

Add a letter to each of these words so that they fit the clue.
Reading down the answers, the added letters spell out the name of one of our feathered friends.

1 Lively
2 Stout, chubby
3 Gloss or emulsion, eg
4 Device to prevent vehicles moving
5 Another name for the jack in a pack of cards
6 Accompany to a place
7 Single piece of sand
8 Babbling stream
9 ___ Beckham, football celebrity

1	RISK
2	PUMP
3	PINT
4	LAMP
5	NAVE
6	RING
7	GRAN
8	BOOK
9	AVID

Solutions to this month's puzzle on next month's puzzle

SOLUTIONS MARCH, 2014

1 A 2 Ay 3 Ray 4 Year 5 Early 6 Replay 7 Parsley 8 Paralyse

28 Monday

29 Tuesday

30 Wednesday

1 Thursday

2 Friday

3 Saturday

4 Sunday

MAY

5 Monday BANK HOLIDAY

6 Tuesday

7 Wednesday

8 Thursday

9 Friday

10 Saturday

11 Sunday

Have a go at..
Appliqué

Layer fabric shapes and stitch in place to create a pretty cupcake picture

YOU WILL NEED

* Various fabric scraps suitable for appliqué plate, cupcake and bunting
* 21.5cm square piece of pink spotted fabric for background
* 23cm square piece of cream fabric for the backing
* 21 x 7.5cm strip of floral fabric for tablecloth (A)
* 12cm length of trim for plate
* 9cm square of wadding
* Ribbon rosebud
* Matching and contrasting sewing thread
* Tracing paper and pencil
* Pins
* Paper and fabric scissors

Designed by textile artist Abigail Mill, this appliqué picture is the ideal project for novices. You can either machine- or hand-stitch the fabric pieces on to the background fabric, then embellish with trimmings and decorative stitching. We've given you patterns for the shapes (below). The appliqué can be framed or used on a bag or a cushion. It's also available as a complete kit (see box, opposite).

To make

1 Enlarge the templates (left) on a photocopier by 200%. Then trace the patterns on to tracing paper, label and cut out.

2 Use the patterns to cut out the plate, cupcake pieces and bunting shapes from your chosen fabric scraps, cutting six bunting pendants in total. Cut the cupcake filling from the wadding. Label fabrics B to F.

3 Position the background fabric centrally on the backing fabric and pin in place. Straight stitch all around,

---

Appliqué pattern templates Enlarge on a photocopier by 200%

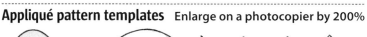

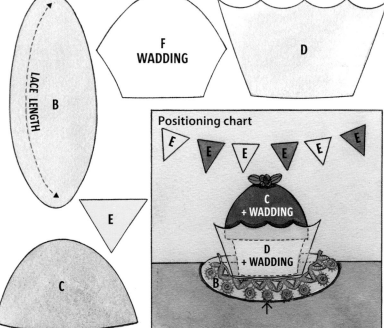

B LACE LENGTH

F
WADDING

D

E

C

Positioning chart

E E E E E E

C
+ WADDING

D
+ WADDING

B

TIPS

✓ The straight stitching on our appliqué was worked on a sewing machine, but it could easily be done by hand. More experienced stitchers could also work freehand machine embroidery on the appliqué — although you would need to stretch the fabric in a hoop if you do it this way.

✓ This is an ideal project for using up fabric scraps.

5mm in from the edge, using matching sewing thread. Position the tablecloth rectangle (A) across the lower edge and straight stitch in place 3mm in from the edge, using a contrasting coloured thread. Don't worry about the accuracy of your stitching as imperfections are all part of the charm of this project.

4 Using our colour photo as a guide and following the positioning chart (opposite), place plate (B) centrally on to the tablecloth, approximately 4cm

up from the lower edge. Then place decorative trim around the plate and pin in position. Put the wadding (F) on top of the plate where the cupcake will sit and pin the sponge (C) over the top section of the wadding.

5 Stitch around the plate using a matching coloured thread, about 3-4mm in from the edge of the motif. Stitch again to secure the trim. Then stitch around the curved top edge of the sponge, about 5mm in from the edge. Position the cupcake case (D) over the cupcake and straight stitch by hand, or machine embroider, in place as shown.

6 Sew the rosebud trim to the top of the cupcake with a few hand stitches.

7 Pin bunting pendants (E), evenly spaced in an arc shape, across the top of the picture. Then, using contrasting thread, straight stitch across the top of the pendants in an arc shape, so that only the top of them are attached. Your appliqué is now ready to frame.

POST – CARD

POST – CARD

World heritage site of Albert Dock in Liverpool

Reader Samantha Priestley, who lives in Sheffield, South Yorkshire, nominates the Albert Dock in Liverpool

'My favourite place is the wonderfully restored Albert Dock in Liverpool. It's a beautiful area to explore at the water's edge and it's packed with shops, museums, art galleries, restaurants and bars. Most of the museums are free, as is the Liverpool Tate, and there's more than enough to keep you busy. But it's also a relaxing place to stroll and breathe in the fresh air.'

Solva in Pembrokeshire

Reader Joan Voyce, from Helensvale in Queensland, Australia, recommends Solva in Pembrokeshire

'Solva is one of the most attractive villages in Wales. It has beautiful coastal walks, charming shops, restaurants, cafés and good pubs, where you can eat fabulous fresh seafood like lobster, crab and mackerel, plus quaint places to have bed and breakfast. There are pleasure boats to take you fishing or just around the nearby islands, such as Skomer, to see the birds and the seals. It's a magical spot!'

12 Monday

13 Tuesday

14 Wednesday

15 Thursday

16 Friday

17 Saturday

18 Sunday

Daisy, daisy. . .

Pretty pastel stripes conjure up a cool, summery sweater

MEASUREMENTS

To fit sizes 81 (86) (91) (97) (102) cm/32 (34) (36) (38) (40) in.
Actual measurements 85 (90.5) (96) (102) (107) cm/ 33½ (35½) (37¾) (40) (42) in.
Side seam 34 (34) (34.5) (35) (36.5) cm/13¼ (13¼) (13½) (13¾) (14¼) in.
Length to shoulder 54.5 (55) (56.5) (57) (59) cm/21½ (21¾) (22¼) (22½) (23¼) in.
Sleeve seam 43 (43) (44.5) (45.5) (46.5) cm/17 (17) (17½) (18) (18¼) in.

MATERIALS

3 (4) (4) (4) (4) 50g balls of RYC Luxury Cotton DK in Blue (Crisp 00253) and 3 (3) (3) (4) (4) balls in each of Lime (Tang 00252), Dark Pink (Slipper 00254), Light Pink (Damsel 00251). No. 8 (4mm) and No. 10 (3¼mm) knitting needles. Yarn costs about £3.50 per 50g ball. For stockists, write to: Rowan Yarns, Green Lane Mill, Holmfirth, West Yorkshire HD7 1RW (01484 681881).

TENSION

22 stitches and 30 rows, to 10 x 10cm, over stocking stitch, using No. 8 (4mm) needles.

ABBREVIATIONS

K, knit; **p,** purl; **st,** stitch; **dec,** decrease (by taking 2 sts together); **inc,** increase (by working twice in same st); **ss,** stocking st (k on right side and p on wrong side).

NOTE

Instructions are given for small size. Where they vary, work figures in round brackets for larger sizes. Instructions in square brackets are worked as stated after 2nd bracket.

BACK

** With No. 10 (3¼mm) needles and Blue, cast on 94 (102) (106) (114) (118) sts.
1st rib row: K2, [p2, k2] to end.
2nd rib row: P2, [k2, p2] to end.
Rib another 4 rows, decreasing 2 sts evenly across last row on 2nd and 4th sizes only — 94 (100) (106) (112) (118) sts.
Change to No. 8 (4mm) needles. Beginning with a k row, work in ss and stripes of 6 rows Lime, 6 rows Dark Pink, 6 rows Light Pink and 6 rows Blue throughout, at the same time, dec 1 st at each end of 17th row and 4 following 6th rows — 84 (90) (96) (102) (108) sts. Ss 9 (9) (11) (13) (17) rows.

Inc 1 st at each end of next row and 4 following 8th rows — 94 (100) (106) (112) (118) sts. Ss another 11 rows.
Shape armholes: Cast off 5 (6) (6) (7) (7) sts at beginning of next 2 rows. Dec 1 st at each end of next 5 (5) (7) (7) (9) rows and 1 (2) (2) (3) (3) following alternate row(s), then on following 4th row — 70 (72) (74) (76) (78) sts. **
Ss another 47 (47) (47) (45) (45) rows.
Shape shoulder and neck: Cast off 6 (6) (7) (7) (7) sts at beginning of next row.
Next row: Cast off 6 (6) (7) (7) (7) sts, p16 (16) (16) (16) (17) sts more, cast off next 24 (26) (26) (28) (28) sts, p to end. Work on

last set of 17 (17) (17) (17) (18) sts for right shoulder.
Right shoulder: Cast off 6 (6) (7) (7) (7) sts at beginning of next row and 4 sts on following row. Cast off remaining 7 (7) (6) (6) (7) sts.
Left shoulder: With right side facing, rejoin yarn to remaining 17 (17) (17) (17) (18) sts and k to end. Cast off 6 (6) (7) (7) (7) sts at beginning of next row and 4 sts on following row. Cast off remaining 7 (7) (6) (6) (7) sts.

FRONT

Work as given for back from ** to **.
Ss another 20 (20) (20) (16) (16) rows.

Shape neck: Next row: P28 (28) (29) (30) (31), cast off next 14 (16) (16) (16) (16) sts, p to end. Work on last set of 28 (28) (29) (30) (31) sts for left half neck.

Left half neck: Dec 1 st at neck edge on next 3 rows and 5 (5) (5) (6) (6) following alternate rows, then on following 4th row — 19 (19) (20) (20) (21) sts. Ss 9 rows.

Shape shoulder: Cast off 6 (6) (7) (7) (7) sts at beginning of next row and following alternate row. P 1 row. Cast off remaining 7 (7) (6) (6) (7) sts.

Right half neck: With right side facing, rejoin yarn to remaining 28 (28) (29) (30) (31) sts and k to end. Dec 1 st at neck edge on next 3 rows and 3 (3) (3) (6) (6) following alternate rows, then on following 4th row — 19 (19) (20) (20) (21) sts. Ss 9 rows.

Shape shoulder: Cast off 6 (6) (7) (7) (7) sts at beginning of next row and following alternate row. K 1 row. Cast off remaining 7 (7) (6) (6) (7) sts.

SLEEVES

(BOTH ALIKE)
With No. 10 (3¼mm) needles and Blue, cast on 50 (50) (50) (54) (54) sts.
Work 2 rows in rib as given for back. Continue in rib in stripes of 2 rows Lime, 2 rows Dark Pink, 2 rows Light Pink, 2 rows Blue and 2 rows Lime, increasing 2 sts evenly across last row on 3rd size only — 50 (50) (52) (54) (54) sts. Change to No. 8 (4mm) needles. Beginning with a k row, work in ss and stripes of 2 rows Dark Pink, 2 rows Light Pink, 2 rows Blue and 2 rows Lime throughout, increasing 1 st at each end of 9th row and 9 (10) (10) (10) (11) following 10th rows — 70 (72) (74) (76) (78) sts.
Ss another 17 (7) (11) (15) (7) rows.

Shape top: Cast off 5 (6) (6) (7) (7) sts at beginning of next 2 rows. Dec 1 st at each end of next row and 5 following 4th rows, then on 8 (8) (9) (9) (10) following alternate rows — 32 sts. Dec 1 st at each end of next 5 rows — 22 sts. Cast off.

NECKBAND

Join right shoulder seam. With right side facing, using Light Pink and No. 10 (3¼mm) needles, pick up and k28 (28) (28) (31) (31) sts down left front neck, 14 (16) (16) (16) (16) sts from centre front, 28 (28) (28) (31) (31) sts up right front neck, 4 sts down right back neck, 24 (26) (26) (28) (28) sts from centre back, then 4 sts up left

back neck — 102 (106) (106) (114) (114) sts. Work in rib as given for back in stripes of 1 row Light Pink, 2 rows Blue, 2 rows Dark Pink, 2 rows Lime and 2 rows Blue. With Blue, cast off in rib.

TO MAKE UP

Join left shoulder and neckband seam. Set in sleeves. Join side and sleeve seams.

This round-neck sweater has set-in sleeves and shaped sides. It's knitted in stocking stitch with double-rib edgings. The yarn is cotton viscose and silk mix, and is hand-wash only.

Your Good Health

Ask Dr Mel

Q I get stomach cramps whenever I'm stressed. How can I stop them?

A You're not alone, according to a recent survey that found that one in three of us gets lower abdominal pain when anxious or under pressure, for example because of arguments with loved ones, money worries or even parking hassles.

Stress releases hormones that affect the muscles in our bowels. These normally contract several times a minute without us noticing, but when we're stressed (or have a tummy bug) they contract more forcefully, so we feel the cramps. If they're severe we may feel faint, nauseated or bloated, and/or need to run to the toilet.

This happens regularly in irritable bowel syndrome, which can be triggered by food intolerance as well as stress. If they only happen when you're stressed, and you're otherwise well, it's unlikely that there's anything seriously wrong. You can buy antispasmodic medication to use when you get the pain, such as mebeverine or Buscopan Cramps (check with your pharmacist as not everyone can take these). But in the longer-term, I'd suggest finding ways to relieve your stress, for example by taking regular exercise, learning relaxation techniques, or changing your lifestyle.

TRY THIS Foot Exercises

*Feet need to be flexible to absorb the shock as they hit the ground when we walk or run — so the muscles, bones and joints should be in good condition. Try these daily exercises: * Sit on a chair or stool and use the sole of one foot to rub up and down the opposite shin from knee to ankle and down again. Repeat 20 times. This helps relieve tension around the shinbone while also increasing the flexibility of the massaging foot. * Holding on to the back of a chair, feet slightly apart, rise up and down on to your tiptoes 10 times. Have a 10-second rest and repeat a*

HEALTH ON MY SHELF
Sian Porter, dietitian

What's in your medicine cabinet?
Magic Cream (from www.magic-cream.co.uk), which aids healing and gives relief, ibuprofen and headache gel.

What's good in your fridge?
Leftover potato, swede and parsnip to mash for salmon fishcakes; 1% fat milk; an eye mask; and some seeds waiting to be sown in our vegetable patch.

What's your favourite exercise?
Walking the dog. He doesn't accept excuses, so you have to do it.

What's a special healthy treat?
Perfectly ripe fruit, particularly mango.

What makes you stressed?
Lack of time, people not telling the truth.

If you can't sleep, what works?
I have a pad and pen by my bed, so I write down what's buzzing around in my head.

Any childhood remedy you still use?
Dock leaves for nettle stings. And a kiss better works for everything!
Sian is consultant dietitian to the potato council.

TAKE 5...
Sleep Better

1 STICK TO A ROUTINE — try to get up and go to bed about the same time every day/night.

2 AVOID caffeine, smoking, and too much food or alcohol in the evening.

3 TAKE REGULAR EXERCISE — but not too near bedtime.

4 WIND DOWN towards bedtime — choose relaxing rather than exciting books or TV.

5 HAVE A WARM BATH and a warm milky drink before bed. Make sure bedroom colours, noise and temperature are restful, and your bed is comfortable.

19 Monday

20 Tuesday

21 Wednesday

22 Thursday

23 Friday

24 Saturday

25 Sunday

Roast Asparagus & Tomato Tart

SERVES *8*
CALORIES *380*
FAT *29g*
SATURATED FAT *16g*
SUITABLE FOR FREEZING *No*

FOR THE PASTRY

* *175g (6oz) plain white flour*
* *Salt and ground black pepper*
* *75g (2½oz) chilled butter*
* *1 medium egg, separated*

FOR THE FILLING

* *100g bunch asparagus tips, about 16 spears, trimmed*
* *8 baby plum tomatoes, halved*
* *1 clove garlic, peeled and finely chopped*
* *A few sprigs of fresh tarragon or oregano*
* *2 tablespoons olive oil*
* *15g (½oz) Parmesan cheese*
* *250g carton mascarpone cheese*
* *4 medium eggs*
* *35 x 12cm (14 x 4½in) tin, or a 23cm (9in) round tin*

1 **To make the pastry:** Sift the flour and a pinch of salt into a bowl. Shave in the butter, then rub it in. Whisk the egg yolk with 3 tablespoons cold water, stir in with a round-bladed knife to make a dough. (Or make pastry in a food processor.) Knead together lightly and form into an oblong. Wrap in cling film, and chill for 30 minutes.

2 Roll out the pastry on a lightly floured surface. Line the tin, bringing the pastry about 5mm (½in) up above the edge. Prick the base, then chill it, while the oven heats up to 200°C or Gas Mark 6. Line the pastry case with baking parchment and baking beans. Bake for 10 minutes near the bottom of the oven.

3 Take out the paper and beans, and bake for another 10 minutes to set the pastry. Beat the egg white and brush a little over the pastry. Put back in the oven for 5 minutes.

4 Meanwhile, put the asparagus and halved tomatoes, skin-side down, on a baking tray. Scatter with garlic and tuck in the tarragon or oregano. Season and drizzle with the oil, and roast for 15 minutes, above the pastry case. Set aside.

5 Lower the oven temperature to 190°C or Gas Mark 5. Sprinkle half the Parmesan on the base of the flan. Beat the mascarpone in a large bowl to soften it, then beat in the eggs with some seasoning. Pour into the flan case, then arrange the asparagus and tomatoes in the flan, pushing them down gently. Sprinkle with the rest of the Parmesan cheese.

6 Bake for 35 minutes until just set. Leave for 5 minutes to cool. Take out of the tin and serve warm or cold, with a salad.

Friends United

Funny, I was never one for crowds before, being a bit shy, but now I've got Bern's health to think of, I've branched out...

I was just giving Bern's hair a bit of a comb, when the doorbell rang. It was Veronica.

She said, "If you can get someone to sit with hubby, Muriel, we're one short for our yoga demo. How about it?"

I said, "Oh, I don't know, Veronica. I like yoga, but in front of people! It's not as if I'm one of the supple ones."

She said, "It's bodies I want. You'll be doing me a favour."

Veronica has been ever so good to me since the accident. It was her wall my Bern had the presence of mind to push me over, when that car swerved towards us. It missed me by inches, but Bern...

I said, "OK, but I must tell the patient first. Dr Chowdry stressed the importance of keeping Bern involved. He says coma victims need as much stimulus as possible and chatting about your day is as good as any."

I rang Trevor, my neighbour. He's been marvellous. A mild-mannered bank manager who wouldn't say boo to a goose, except at weekends. He does his battle re-enactments then. There is one drawback, apparently. Lack of female company. By all accounts the majority of wives, girlfriends, etc, prefer spending their weekends doing a bit of retail therapy and pampering, as opposed to cooking over a camp fire dressed in a pinny and cloth cap. He's asked any number of female colleagues from the bank to accompany him. It's always, "Thanks, but no thanks." One or two actually laughed out loud. He can't understand it.

Veronica is pinning her hopes on this publicity stunt. She's been trying to promote Yoga For The Unsupple for months. Tried all the usual avenues, putting up posters, giving out flyers and now this latest venture, performing in front of an audience of amused shoppers. One or two of the ladies are revelling in it, actually.

Uh-oh, there's Dr Chowdry and his wife. Lovely sari she's wearing.

"Hi, Doctor, I'm just..."

"No need to explain, Muriel. I'm a practising yogi myself but I prefer the privacy of my study."

Mrs Chowdry gives me a cheery wave and they go into Bhs.

I'm sure I heard giggling.

Veronica is over the moon. Our little demonstration has brought in two new people. A retired army Major who misses his unit and a shopaholic who made herself known to Veronica after the demo.

Apparently, she's got sixty-three new handbags at home, some of them still in the wrapping.

Veronica has recommended yoga by way of a diversion.

She said she'll certainly give our group a try and, when she gets home, she's going straight onto eBay to buy a new mat.

I invited everyone over to my place on Sunday. Cheese and wine. We're having Bern's favourite, Stilton. He can't eat any, of course, but I'm positive the company will do him good.

Funny, I was never one for crowds of people before, being a bit on the shy side, but now I've got Bern's health to think of, I've branched out.

Trevor popped in after his meet, still wearing his armour. Says he likes to keep in character for a few hours, helps him unwind. We didn't mind, but Veronica said he got quite bossy when she passed the coffees around. It's so unlike him. Must be the uniform.

Marks and Spencer's most loyal customer is pleased. She's been telling Bern all about her marital problems etcetera and the upshot of it is, she's been able to walk in and out of the shop without purchasing even one handbag. She says chatting to Bern has proved to be the best counselling session she's ever had.

Bit of a breakthrough this week. The Major was getting to a rather exciting point about his old Army days, when he thought he saw Bern's eyelids flicker. We all cheered when he said it. I couldn't stop thanking him actually.

He said, "On the contrary, dear lady, it should be me thanking you."

Turns out that, as a direct result of reliving all his stories, he doesn't miss his unit at all.

I called Dr Chowdry last night. He came over in a jiffy. He took one look at Bern and said, "Muriel, it's out of our hands. It could go either way. We must just be patient."

House is so quiet. Veronica rang. They're missing me at the group. Said they're running to capacity now, two to a mat. When am I coming back?

I said, "I don't know. What with Bern..."

She said, "No arguments, the group will be round as usual and what's more, I'm bring the cheese and wine."

Oh, we've had such a party! Stilton all round and I mean all round.

Dr Chowdry said he's never known a wake-up like it. Says he's sure it's because Bern has been surrounded with friends all these weeks.

I said, "We're the friends united and what's more, it's been a wake up call for all of us."

THE END
© Margaret Potter, 2008

She said, 'It's bodies I want. You'll be doing me a favour'

26 Monday SPRING BANK HOLIDAY

27 Tuesday

28 Wednesday

29 Thursday

30 Friday

31 Saturday

1 Sunday

NUMBER JIG

All you have to do is fit these numbers into the grid, reading across and down.

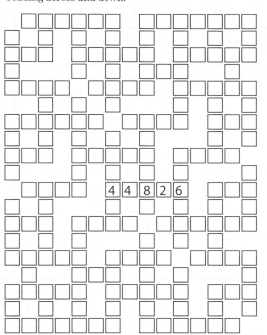

3 DIGITS	4 DIGITS	5 DIGITS	6 DIGITS
101	1111	12962	166573
122	1135	14146	340480
155	1836	31525	366763
158	1875	35636	384421
208	2700	44826	566881
247	3077	50480	680420
364	3460	51837	746615
366	3585	58378	943036
415	5086	60880	948159
417	5356	62588	975741
438	5385	65888	
534	5625	72724	**7 DIGITS**
604	6451	74331	1647256
635	7548	80128	2676264
683	8817		4477675
966	9146		5362406

CODEWORD

A grid of numbered cells forming a crossword pattern, with the following letter clues filled in: 12=A, 20=R, 10=C.

| A̶ | B | C̶ | D | E | F | G | H | I | J | K | L | M | N | O | P | Q | R̶ | S | T | U | V | W | X | Y | Z̶ |

1	2	3	4	5	6	7	8	9	10 **C**	11	12 **A**	13
14	15	16	17	18	19	20 **R**	21	22	23	24	25	26

Solutions to this month's puzzle on next month's puzzle

SOLUTIONS FOR APRIL, 2014

ACROSS 1 Side **3** Aspersions **10** Aisle **11** Utterance **12** Hornpipe **13** Bedeck **15** Noddy **16** Lordship **19** Starters **21** Gaffe **23** Onions **25** Masseuse **27** Molehills **28** Ernie **29** Last resort **30** Rest
DOWN 1 Scathing **2** Discredit **4** Slug pellet **5** Eats **6** Surveys **7** Ounce **8** Sheikh **9** Deeply **14** Trespasser **17** Influence **18** Reverent **20** Rancher **21** Gospel **22** Normal **24** Isles **26** Alas

BLACKBIRD

JUNE

Frozen Strawberry & Chocolate Slice

SERVES *6-8*
CALORIES *634*
FAT *46g*
SATURATED FAT *29g*
SUITABLE FOR FREEZING *Yes*

INGREDIENTS
* 600ml carton double cream
* 250g (8oz) icing sugar
* A few drops of vanilla extract

FOR THE STRAWBERRY MIXTURE
* 250g (8oz) strawberries
* 2 tablespoons caster sugar

FOR THE CHOCOLATE LAYER
* 200g bar plain chocolate, melted
* Strawberries, to decorate
* 1kg (2lb) loaf tin, or mould, preferably silicone
* 2 x large, disposable piping bags

1 Pour the cream into a bowl, add the icing sugar and a few drops of vanilla extract, and whip until it forms soft peaks.

2 Purée the strawberries with the caster sugar and then fold in half of the cream mixture.

3 Divide the remaining cream mixture in half. Keep one half plain, then gradually stir the other half into the melted chocolate (add the cream gradually, so the chocolate doesn't set too quickly).

4 Pour a thin layer of the strawberry mixture into the base of the loaf tin and freeze it until solid. Then, fill a piping bag with the plain cream mixture and cut off the end of the bag to give a hole about 2cm (¾in) in diameter. Pipe balls all over the strawberry layer. Freeze until solid.

5 Remove the pan from the freezer and pour over a strawberry-cream layer to cover the white balls. Put back in the freezer and freeze until it's solid.

6 Fill the other piping bag with chocolate mixture and cut off the end of the bag to give a hole about 2cm (¾in) in diameter. Pipe balls all over the strawberry ice. Freeze until the chocolate balls are solid. Remove it from the freezer and pour over the remaining strawberry mixture. Freeze until solid.

7 Remove from the freezer and turn the slice out of the mould on to a serving plate: If using a silicone mould, it just needs peeling away; if it's a metal tin, dip it briefly into hot water, dry the tin and then tip the slice out on to a plate. Decorate with halved strawberries before serving.

8 Once frozen, wrap the tin in a freezer bag and keep frozen for up to 1 month.

TIP FROM OUR KITCHEN
Make sure each layer is
completely frozen before adding
the next so that the layers
don't mix together.

Your Good Health

Ask Dr Mel

Q I've been diagnosed with sciatica. What's the best treatment?

A Sciatica is a pain that starts in the buttock, spreading down the back of the leg and under the foot; sometimes it causes numbness as well. The most common cause is compression of the sciatic nerve, which leaves the spinal cord in the lower back and controls movement and feeling in this area; if it's damaged, it sends faulty signals to the brain, which "thinks" there's something wrong with the leg itself. Trapping may be due to arthritis or a fracture in the spinal bones (vertebrae) or rupture of the gristly shock-absorbing disc between two vertebrae.

A recent British analysis of worldwide research has found that the most effective drugs are NSAIDs (non-steroidal anti-inflammatory drugs), muscle relaxants such as diazepam, and/or small regular doses of the antidepressant amitriptyline rather than morphine-related (opioid) drugs, although you may find paracetamol and/or codeine effective. Stay as active as you can, and have physiotherapy, which may "untrap" the nerve. If symptoms persist, you'll need an MR scan to see whether spinal surgery would help. Researchers also recommend injections of steroids into the epidural space around the nerve in the spine.

TRY THIS Leg Toning

To exercise your quads (the front of your thighs), sit in an upright chair and raise one foot so that your leg is straight, hold for three seconds, then bring back to the floor. Repeat 10 times each side. To exercise the hamstrings (back of the thighs), again take a seated position but this time pull a foot underneath you, close to your bottom. Repeat 10 times each side. Personal trainer John Byers says that you'll get more out of these simple exercises if you use ankle weights. "Be sure to maintain good posture by keeping your head and chest upright."

HEALTH ON MY SHELF
Joanne Sumner, yoga, reiki and meditation practitioner

What's in your medicine cabinet?
Healing Herbs Five Natural Flower Cream with calendula, for skin complaints; and lavender essential oil for headaches.
What's good in your fridge?
Red berries, peppers, carrots, courgettes — I like food to be colourful, because then I know I'm getting a range of nutrients.
What's your favourite exercise?
Yoga. It helps me focus, stretches my body and gets my energy flowing.
If you can't sleep, what works?
I breathe in lightly through the crown of my head and down to my feet, and breathe out back up the body.
What stresses you?
Not having enough time to myself. I meditate for a few minutes each day.
Any childhood remedy you still use?
I find colouring in a great soother.
For details about Joanne Sumner's retreats, visit www.joannesumner.com.

TAKE 5...
Symptoms You Shouldn't Ignore

1 CHEST PAIN — usually feels tight or heavy at the front of the chest and may spread to the arms or neck. Dial 999 if it lasts more than ten minutes.

2 UNDUE SHORTNESS OF BREATH when resting or exercising, or waking you from sleep.

3 PALPITATIONS — fast and/or irregular heart beats, often felt as thudding or the heart racing.

4 UNEXPLAINED DIZZINESS or loss of consciousness.

5 ANKLE SWELLING — may be a sign of heart failure.

2 Monday

3 Tuesday

4 Wednesday

5 Thursday

6 Friday

7 Saturday

8 Sunday

Orange Crush

We love vibrant citrus shades in the summer months, and this lace-up cardi is an easy way to work the look

MEASUREMENTS

To fit sizes 76 (81) (87) (91) (97) (102) (107) (112) cm/30 (32) (34) (36) (38) (40) (42) (44) in.
Actual measurements 81 (85) (90.5) (96) (101) (107) (110.5) (116) cm/32 (33½) (35½) (37¾) (39¾) (42) (43½) (45¾) in.
Side seam 28 (28.5) (29.5) (30) (30.5) (31.5) (32) (32.5) cm/11 (11¼) (11½) (11¾) (12) (12¼) (12½) (12¾) in.
Length to shoulder 46 (47.5) (48.5) (50) (51.5) (52.5) (54) (55.5) cm/18 (18¾) (19) (19¾) (20¼) (20¾) (21¼) (21¾) in.
Sleeve seam 41.5 (42) (42.5) (43.5) (44) (44.5) (45.5) (46) cm/16¼ (16½) (16¾) (17) (17¼) (17½) (17¾) (18) in.

MATERIALS

Pair of 3¼mm (No. 10) and 4mm (No. 8) knitting needles; size 3.00 crochet hook. One 500g cone of Yeoman DK Soft Cotton (100-per-cent cotton). Yarn is available by mail order only and costs £14.95 per 500g cone, including p&p. We used Tango, but the yarn is also available in White, Cream, Sugar, Lilac, Black, Denim, Lime and Turquoise. To order, or for a free shade card, write to Yeoman Yarns Ltd, 36 Churchill Way, Fleckney, Leicestershire LE8 8UD, call 0116 240 4464, email sales@yeomanyarns.co.uk or visit www.yeoman-yarns.co.uk.

TENSION

22 stitches and 30 rows, to 10 x 10cm, over stocking stitch, using 4mm needles.

ABBREVIATIONS

K, knit; **p,** purl; **st,** stitch; **tog,** together; **dec,** decrease (by working 2 sts tog); **inc,** increase (by working twice into same st); **ss,** stocking st (k on right side and p on wrong side); **gst,** garter st (every row k); **skpo,** slip 1, k1, pass slip st over; **up1,** pick up loop lying between needles and k or p into the back of it; **yf,** yarn forward to make a st.

NOTE

Yarn amounts are based on average requirements and are approximate. Instructions are for small size. Where they vary, work figures in round brackets for larger sizes. Instructions in square brackets are worked as stated after 2nd bracket.

BACK

With 3¼mm needles, cast on 89 (93) (99) (105) (111) (117) (121) (127) sts.
1st rib row: K1, [p1, k1] to end.
2nd rib row: P1, [k1, p1] to end. Rib another 2 rows.
Change to 4mm needles.
Beginning with a k row, ss 5 rows.
Marker row: P22 (23) (25) (27) (29) (31) (32) (34), mark last st, p to last 21 (22) (24) (26) (28) (30) (31) (33) sts, mark last st, p to end.
1st dec row: [K to within 2 sts of marked st, skpo, k marked st, k2tog] twice, k to end. Ss 5 (5) (5) (5) (7) (7) (7) (7) rows. Repeat last 6 (6) (6) (6) (8) (8) (8) (8) rows, once more, then 1st dec row again — 77 (81) (87) (93) (99) (105) (109) (115) sts. Ss another 11 (13) (15) (17) (15) (17) (9) (11) rows.
Increase row: K to 1st marked st, up1, k to 2nd marked st, k marked st, up1, k to end. Ss 5 (5) (5) (5) (5) (5) (7) (7) rows. Repeat last 6 (6) (6) (6) (6) (6) (8) (8) rows, 4 times more, then increase row again — 89 (93) (99) (105) (111) (117) (121) (127) sts. Ss another 19 rows.
Shape armholes: Cast off 3 (3) (4) (4) (5) (6) (6) (6) sts at beginning of next 2 rows.
2nd dec row: K4, skpo, k to last 6 sts, k2tog, k4. P 1 row. Repeat last 2 rows, 4 (5) (5) (6) (6) (7) (7) (8) times more, then 2nd dec row again — 71 (73) (77) (81) (85) (87) (91) (95) sts. Ss another 41 (41) (43) (43) (45) (45) (47) (47) rows.
Shape shoulder: Next row: Cast off 16 (17) (17) (19) (20) (21) (21) (23) sts, k to last 16 (17) (17) (19) (20) (21) (21) (23) sts, cast off last 16 (17) (17) (19) (20) (21) (21) (23) sts. Leave remaining 39 (39) (43) (43) (45) (45) (49) (49) sts on a st holder.

LEFT FRONT

With 3¼mm needles, cast on 45 (47) (49) (53) (55) (59) (61) (63) sts.
1st rib row: [K1, p1] to last 3 sts, k3.
2nd rib row: K2, p1, [k1, p1] to end. Rib another 2 rows, increasing 1 st at centre of last row on 3rd, 5th and 8th sizes only — 45 (47) (50) (53) (56) (59) (61) (64) sts.
Change to 4mm needles.
1st row: K to end. **2nd row:** K2, p to end. Keeping the 2 sts at front edge in gst and remainder in ss and making eyelet holes at front edge on 11th (15th) (1st) (5th) (3rd) (7th) (9th) (13th) row and 8 (8) (8) (8) (10) (10) (10) (10) following 10th (10th) (12th) (12th) (10th) (10th) (10th) (10th) rows thus: k to last 4 sts, skpo, yf, k2, at the same time, continue as follows: Work 3 rows.
Marking row: K2, p22 (23) (24) (25) (26) (27) (28) (29),

mark last st, p to end.
** 1st dec row: K to within 2 sts of marked st, skpo, k marked st, k2tog, k to end. Ss 5 (5) (5) (5) (7) (7) (7) (7) rows. Repeat last 6 (6) (6) (6) (8) (8) (8) (8) rows, once more, then 1st dec row again — 39 (41) (44) (47) (50) (53) (55) (58) sts. Work another 11 (13) (15) (17) (15) (17) (9) (11) rows.
Increase row: K to marked st — k marked st on right front — up1, k to end. Ss 5 (5) (5) (5) (5) (5) (7) (7) rows. Repeat last 6 (6) (6) (6) (6) (6) (8) (8) rows, 4 times more, then increase row again — 45 (47) (50) (53) (56) (59) (61) (64) sts. **
Work another 19 rows.
Shape armhole: Cast off 3 (3) (4) (4) (5) (6) (6) (6) sts at beginning of next row. Work 1 row.
2nd dec row: K4, skpo, k to end. Work 1 row. Repeat last 2 rows, 5 (6) (6) (7) (7) (8) (8) (9) times more — 36 (37) (39) (41) (43) (44) (46) (48) sts.
Shape neck: Next row: K to last 6 (6) (6) (6) (7) (7) (7) (7) sts, turn and leave the 6 (6) (6) (6) (7) (7) (7) (7) sts on a safety-pin — 30 (31) (33) (35) (36) (37) (39) (41) sts.
*** P 1 row. Work 1st dec row. Ss 3 rows. Repeat last 4 rows, 5 (5) (6) (6) (6) (6) (7) (7) times more, then work 1st dec row again — 16 (17) (17) (19) (20) (21) (21) (23) sts. Ss another 13 (13) (11) (11) (13) (13) (11) (11) rows. Cast off. ***

RIGHT FRONT

With 3¼mm needles, cast on 45 (47) (49) (53) (55) (59) (61) (63) sts.
1st rib row: K3, [p1, k1] to end.
2nd rib row: [P1, k1] to last 3 sts, p1, k2. Rib another 2 rows, increasing 1 st at centre of last row on 3rd, 5th and 8th sizes only — 45 (47) (50) (53) (56) (59) (61) (64) sts. Change to 4mm needles.
1st row: K to end. **2nd row:** P to last 2 sts, k2. Keeping the 2 sts at

front edge in gst and remainder in ss and making eyelet holes at front edge on 11th (15th) (1st) (5th) (3rd) (7th) (9th) (13th) row and 8 (8) (8) (8) (10) (10) (10) (10) following 10th (10th) (12th) (12th) (10th) (10th) (10th) (10th) rows thus: k2, yf, k2tog, k to end, at the same time, continue as follows: Work 3 rows.

Marking row: P22 (23) (25) (27) (29) (31) (32) (34), mark last st, p to last 2 sts, k2.
Work as left front from ** to **, noting variation. Work another 20 rows.
Shape armhole: Cast off 3 (3) (4) (4) (5) (6) (6) (6) sts at beginning of next row.
2nd dec row: K to last 6 sts, k2tog, k4. Work 1 row. Repeat last 2 rows, 5 (6) (6) (7) (7) (8) (8) (9) times more — 36 (37) (39) (41) (43) (44) (46) (48) sts.
Shape neck: Next row: K6 (6) (6) (6) (7) (7) (7) (7) and leave these sts on a safety-pin, k to end — 30 (31) (33) (35) (36) (37) (39) (41) sts.
Work as left front from *** to ***.

SLEEVES (BOTH ALIKE)

With 3¼mm needles, cast on 41 (43) (45) (47) (49) (51) (53) (55) sts. Rib 4 rows as on back. Change to 4mm needles.
Increase row: K4, up1, k to last 4 sts, up1, k4. Ss 7 rows. Repeat last 8 rows, 13 (13) (13) (13) (14) (14) (14) (14) times more, then increase row again — 71 (73) (75) (77) (81) (83) (85) (87) sts. Ss another 7 (9) (11) (13) (7) (9) (11) (13) rows.
Shape top: Cast off 3 (3) (4) (4) (5) (6) (6) (6) sts at beginning of next 2 rows. Dec 1 st at each end of next row and following 4th row, then on next 7 (8) (10) (11) (10) (12) (13) (14) alternate rows — 47 (47) (43) (43) (47) (43) (43) (43) sts. P 1 row. Dec 1 st at each end of next 10 (10) (8) (8) (10) (8) (8) (8) rows — 27 sts. Cast off 4 sts at beginning of next 2 rows — 19 sts. Cast off.

NECKBAND

Join shoulder seams. With right side facing and using 3¼mm needles, slip 6 (6) (6) (6) (7) (7) (7) (7) sts from right front safety-pin onto needle, pick up and k30 (30) (32) (32) (34) (34) (36) (36) sts up right front neck, k39 (39) (43) (43) (45) (45) (49) (49) sts from back neck, pick up and k30 (30) (32) (32) (34) (34) (36) (36) sts down left front neck, then k6 (6) (6) (6) (7) (7) (7) (7) sts from left front safety-pin — 111 (111) (119) (119) (127) (127) (135) (135) sts.
1st rib row: K3, [p1, k1] to last 4 sts, p1, k3.
2nd rib row: K2, p1, [k1, p1] to last 2 sts, k2.
Rib 1 row. Cast off in rib.

TO MAKE UP

Sew in sleeves, then join side and sleeve seams. Crochet chain 150cm long and thread through eyelet holes.

POST – CARD

Valencia in Spain

Reader Margaret Young, from Oxford, recommends Valencia in Spain

'Valencia is a city of contrasts. The Old City is known for the Las Fallas celebrations in spring, but it also has a 12th-century cathedral and a colourful market. In contrast, a walk along the dried riverbed, passing orange trees and flower-decorated bridges, brings you to Valencia's City of Arts and Sciences, with its amazing bright white buildings. It's a city to enjoy whatever your age.'

POST – CARD

Delgatie Castle in Aberdeenshire

Reader Jo Maley, from Macduff in Aberdeenshire, nominates Delgatie Castle

'I like visiting beautiful Delgatie Castle, which is only about eight miles from where I live, in the coastal town of Macduff. It's a proper, traditional castle, and it has delightful gardens with a peaceful pond, a gift shop and even a "Laird's Kitchen" tea room. The tranquillity of the setting is magical at all times of year, whether it be a hot summer's day or Christmas time.'

9 Monday

10 Tuesday

11 Wednesday

12 Thursday

13 Friday

14 Saturday

15 Sunday

Have a go at..
Making Silver Jewellery

Use silver clay and simple techniques to create these pretty earrings and pendant

YOU WILL NEED

* 10g silver metal clay (see below)
* Olive oil
* Cling film
* Acrylic roller
* Texture mat or rubber stamp (see below)
* Non-stick surface — eg, piece of plastic cut from a plastic stationery folder
* Two 14 x 2.5cm strips of card, each 2mm thick
* 27mm- and 15mm-wide heart metal cutters
* Cocktail stick
* Sanding sponge or fine sandpaper
* Needle file
* Stainless-steel mesh
* Soft brass brush
* Polishing cloth
* 3 sterling-silver pendant bails with loops at the top
* 3 sterling-silver jump rings
* Sterling-silver chain necklace
* Pair of sterling-silver ear wires
* Flat-nosed jewellery pliers

Art Clay Silver 650, £23.80 for 10g (enough to make our pendant and earrings), texture mats, tools and firing, sanding and polishing materials are all available from Metal Clay Ltd (01929 481541; www. metalclay.co.uk). The sterling silver findings and pliers can be bought from Beadworks Bead Shop (020 7240 0931; www.beadworks.co.uk).

Silver clay is fun to use and, like most clays, it can be easily shaped and manipulated. We used heart-shaped cutters and a texture mat to make our jewellery, but you can use any shape of cutter or cut your own design directly from the clay. You can decorate its surface by pressing it with textured objects such as rubber stamps, coins or mesh. You can also etch marks in the clay with a cocktail stick or pin.

WHAT IS SILVER CLAY?

The clay is actually made of tiny particles of pure silver mixed with organic binders and water. It is designed to be fired at a low temperature, so is suitable for home use, as it can be fired on a gas hob (or, for larger pieces, with a gas torch). Once fired, the clay is 99.9% silver, and isn't prone to tarnish. Gold, bronze and copper clays are also available.

FINISHED SIZES: Large heart: 2.5 x 2.5cm; small heart: 13 x 14mm

To make

place it on a non-stick surface with the two 2mm-thick strips of card on either side. Roll the clay, resting the ends of the roller on the card strips, to flatten the clay evenly to a thickness of 2mm.

2 Remove the card strips. Press the texture mat firmly on to the clay to make an impression. Peel off the mat to reveal your design.

1 To prevent the acrylic roller, texture mat and cutting edge of the cutters sticking to the clay, first smooth olive oil sparingly over them. Wrap the clay in cling film and knead it for a few seconds to soften it. Next,

TIPS

✓ If a hole in the clay is too small after firing, enlarge it with a needle file.

✓ Make sure that you read all the clay manufacturer's instructions before you start. The clay must be bone-dry before firing or it can "pop" and burst. For safety, a stainless-steel mesh cage can be placed over the clay as you fire it. Doing this on a gas hob is only suitable for pieces that are no larger than a 50p coin.

6 To fire the clay: Put the large heart on a sheet of stainless-steel mesh. Place the mesh on a gas hob burner and turn on the heat fully. The clay will smoke for a few seconds. Continue to heat the clay for ten minutes, watching it all the time. Turn off the heat and leave the heart to cool completely. The clay will be white after firing. Repeat for the small hearts.

7 Brush the fired metal in a circular motion to achieve a silver satin finish. Give the metal a final rub with a polishing cloth to highlight the raised areas.

clay. Repeat for the small hearts. The clay will shrink by 8-10% during firing, so make sure that all the holes are large enough to accommodate their fixings.

3 Press the large heart cutter firmly on to the clay. Pull away the excess and lift off the cutter. Re-roll and texture this clay and use it to make two small hearts for earrings in the same way, but with the 15mm cutter. Wrap any clay you don't need in cling film straight away and store in an airtight container.

4 Use the cocktail stick to make a small hole at the centre top of the large heart, for hanging. Wiggle the stick so that it goes right through the

5 Leave the pieces for at least 24 hours — until they're completely dry. Handle the clay gently, as it will be brittle. Gently smooth any rough edges with a sanding sponge. Neaten the edges of the holes with a needle file. Take time sanding, as imperfections will show once the metal is fired. You'll still be able to sand after firing, but it's much easier to do it at this stage.

To finish

Slip the prongs of a pendant bail through each hole on the hearts. Close the prongs by gently squeezing the bail between the jaws of the pair of flat-nosed pliers.

For the pendant: Slip a jump ring through the loop of the large heart's bail and then through the middle link of a silver chain necklace. Close the ring with the pliers.

For the earrings: Open the loop of an ear wire and slip it on to the loop of a small heart's bail. Use the pliers as before to close the ring. Repeat to make second earring.

Growing Pains

Her son had a habit of abandoning things when something newer came along: cars; old mobile phones; women...

It was on a Tuesday morning in April that Kate first noticed the bird's nest in Jonathan's car. It nestled between the front seats just behind the handbrake and contained four blue, speckled eggs.

'Blackbird's eggs,' Kate thought.

The car had been in the back garden so long, the blackbird obviously thought it was a permanent fixture. Its windows were open to the elements. Jonathan had left it like that one icy winter day back in February, saying he needed a part.

Then he'd moved out, swiftly and with very little notice, as was his habit, into the home of his latest girlfriend. "She's definitely the one, Mum."

"I'm pleased for you," she said, even though she knew he'd be back inside six months. He had a habit of abandoning things when something newer and shinier came along: cars; old mobile phones; women.

The latest girlfriend was called Hannah and had a little boy. Kate hoped she'd get to meet them one day, but she had a feeling she wouldn't.

Meanwhile, the car deteriorated slowly in the garden. Twigs and leaves found their final resting places on the seats, and finally the blackbird set up home there.

Kate shook her head. She should have asked Jonathan to move it before. Now they would have to wait until the eggs were hatched.

Jonathan turned up again in May.

"Hi, Mum. Sorry I haven't been in touch." He gave her a melting, blue-eyed smile that he'd perfected when he was six. She should have been tougher when he was a boy.

"Things didn't work out with Hannah then?"

"It went a bit stale."

Kate had to bite her lip to stop herself saying, "When will you learn? There's more to a relationship than the buzz of the novelty factor. Life is a series of repetitive actions. Of course it'll get stale."

"We had a massive row."

"I'm sorry."

"Me too," he said, and perhaps he'd caught some of her unsaid words, because he looked it.

Later, she showed him the baby blackbirds and the mother shovelling food into their yawning, outstretched beaks. "Isn't she amazing?" she said. "She goes backwards and forwards all day."

He'd moved out, swiftly and with very little notice

"No Daddy Blackbird helping out then?" His voice was unusually thoughtful.

"Not that I've seen."

He'd been back a week when a tired-eyed woman with long blonde hair and oversized silver hoop earrings turned up on the doorstep. Kate knew immediately it was Hannah, even before she saw the little boy in the car behind her.

No one had ever tracked him down before.

"Jonathan isn't here right now. Was he expecting you?"

"I shouldn't think so." Hannah held out a hand with delicate pink fingernails that contradicted the steeliness in her brown eyes. "Would it be possible for us to come in and wait for him? We've unfinished business."

"Um, yes," Kate said.

A few minutes later, they were installed in her kitchen; Hannah sipping tea and Ben drinking orange squash from a plastic mug with a curly straw that had once belonged to Jonathan. Maybe he got his hoarding tendencies from her.

When he came in a little while later, they were chatting animatedly about *Mamma Mia* and the empowerment of older women.

He paused in the doorway and Kate wondered what he made of the little tableau in the kitchen. She saw his Adam's apple jerk up and down, and then he came across the room. "Hannah. It's good to see you. I'm sorry..."

She put up a hand to stop him. "We both know it's me who should be apologising. I shouldn't have said what I did."

"I don't blame you for saying it. I haven't exactly got a brilliant track record."

Kate waited for Jonathan to say Hannah was too good for him, she deserved someone better, a glib line she'd heard him use many times in the past, but he didn't.

"I meant what I said. I wouldn't walk away from my own child. I'm not the same as Ben's father."

"I know you're not. Now I've had time to think. I was scared, Jonathan. I wondered if we could start again. Be a family like you wanted. If you can forgive the awful things I said?"

Kate wanted to apologise too — for not realising he'd grown up somewhere along the line.

But she was still getting over the shock that she was to be a grandmother; the glorious, heart-churning shock.

Outside the kitchen window, she saw the blackbird, tirelessly performing the endless rituals of parenthood.

She stood up. "Why don't I make us all another cuppa?" she said.

THE END
© Della Galton

16 Monday

17 Tuesday

18 Wednesday

19 Thursday

20 Friday

21 Saturday

22 Sunday

KRISS KROSS

All you have to do is fit these words into the grid, reading across and down.

4 LETTERS
GOLF
YOGA

5 LETTERS
BINGO
DARTS

6 LETTERS
BALLET
CINEMA
CRAFTS
TRAVEL

7 LETTERS
COOKERY
CYCLING
JOGGING
POTTERY
THEATRE

8 LETTERS
AEROBICS
PAINTING

9 LETTERS
GARDENING
GENEALOGY

10 LETTERS
ICE-SKATING
NEEDLEWORK

11 LETTERS
CAMPANOLOGY
CARAVANNING

Solutions to this month's puzzle on next month's puzzle

WORDSEARCH

Find all the listed stationery items in the grid except one — they run either forwards or backwards, horizontally, vertically or diagonally, but always in a straight, unbroken line. The missing word is your answer.

```
L W J H U R E D N I B G N I R
A E S C F B P H A F S T A M P
B P H N E A A I D N O Y A R C
E O A U L L T G H R U L E R P
L L R P T L G H E L I F D I R
N E P E T P N L S T A P L E R
I V E L I O I I I M W S K E R
P N N O P I K G V U S C L S S
G E E H P N C H E T I A T T D
N R R P E T A T N T S R A I R
I D A O N C P E S T I T A E E
W R M P H I M R I N I R S Y D
A A E A H I A C G O Y I J D D
R C R K L P B T N L N D O I E
D T I P R A A E N A U G T T R
S S M N N A R P G U U E T K H
O O G D K Y M R E N O T E S S
C P V A S R O T A R O F R E P
O Y N O T I C E B O A R D D M
```

ADHESIVE
BALLPOINT
CARTRIDGE
CHART
COMPLIMENTS SLIP
CRAYON
DESK TIDY
DIARY
DRAWING-PIN
ELASTIC BAND
ENVELOPE
FELT-TIP PEN
FILE

FOLDER
FOUNTAIN PEN
GLUE
GRAPH PAPER
HIGHLIGHTER
HOLE PUNCH
INK
JOTTER
LABEL
MARKER
NOTEPAD
NOTICEBOARD
ORGANISER
PACKING TAPE

PERFORATOR
POSTCARD
RING BINDER
RULER
SHARPENER
SHREDDER
STAMP
STAPLER
STATIONERY
STICKER
STRING
TAG
TONER

SOLUTIONS MAY, 2014

23 Monday

24 Tuesday

25 Wednesday

26 Thursday

27 Friday

28 Saturday

29 Sunday

JULY

30 Monday

1 Tuesday

2 Wednesday

3 Thursday

4 Friday

5 Saturday

6 Sunday

Take A Doily

So pretty and feminine, doilies are the perfect embellishment to transform items around the home into something special

Pretty As A Picture

Doilies are works of art in themselves — try framing one or using one on a greetings card to give a lovely result.

FRAMED PICTURE
Finished size: 25 x 25cm frame. Cover the backing board of your chosen frame with coloured paper (we used a cornflower blue), and choose a good-sized doily to fit nicely inside your frame. Depending on the size of your doily, either trace off, enlarge or decrease the bird on a branch template (below) and cut from the same paper as the background. Glue the doily to the backing board, then glue the bird to the centre of the doily. Replace the backing board in the frame.

CARD
Finished size: 13.5 x 13.5cm. Carefully cut out the centre of a small doily, keeping it intact. Trace off the bird motif (below) and enlarge or decrease, altering the number of leaves, depending on the size of the centre of your doily, and cut from the cut-out doily centre. Cut a square of blue paper, smaller than the card blank, and finish two opposite edges with scalloped scissors. Glue the doily and bird to the blue square and then glue to the card front.

TIP
If you have a steady hand, try tracing the template on to the centre of the doily and cut out as one whole shape, using a small pair of craft scissors.

Trace off this bird template for the "Pretty as a picture" cards (above)

All Wrapped Up

Doilies make a delicate embellishment for gifts. Just choose an appropriate-size doily for whatever you're wrapping.

PRESENT
Wrap your present in plain paper (we used lilac crêpe paper), then position a large doily over the top, so that the edges hang over the sides, and glue in place. Layer ribbons in toning colours, to complete the look.

GIFT BAG
Either using a shop-bought or a handmade gift bag, fold a heart-shaped doily and place over the top of the bag. Glue down the point of the heart to the front of the bag, then tie a pretty ribbon to hold the doily in place and seal the bag.

THANK-YOU POSY
Wash a jam jar (preferably a smooth one with no ridges) and leave to dry. Choose a suitably-sized doily for the jar, and either neatly write or stamp "thank you" in the centre. Following the manufacturer's instructions, and working in a well-ventilated area, apply spray adhesive to the back of the doily, wait until tacky, then position on the side, smoothing out any air bubbles. Add three lengths of ribbon and complete with a pretty bow. Fill the jar with flowers.

Doilies, from a selection at Poppy's Cabin and Lakeland. Ribbons, from a selection at John Lewis and Paperchase

TIPS
✓ Wrap presents in plain paper, to make the doily stand out; patterned paper can make the overall effect look messy.
✓ Alter the message on the posy jam jar for any occasion — "congratulations", "happy birthday" or even "get well soon".

Well Contained

Plain glass is an ideal surface to stick a doily to for a tea-light holder or a larger container. Choose an appropriate-size doily or cut one up.

GLASS JAR
Following the posy vase instructions (above), apply a large doily to the side of the jar, and one to the lid, if it's wide and flat enough.

TEA-LIGHT
To decorate, cut a small doily in half and use a glue stick to attach it to the holder. Make sure that the edge of doily is flush with the base of the holder. Cut up a doily, following its pattern, to make a flower shape, and glue down, trimming any overhanging edges. Never leave a lit candle unattended.

Tall glass jar, £6.95, Dotcomgiftshop. Kilner jar, £2.99, Attic. Tea-light holders, 99p each, HobbyCraft. Candles, £1.75 each, Wax Lyrical

POST – CARD

Dublin

June Dunphy, from Dumbarton, recommends the city of Dublin

'Family connections meant I was often taken to visit Dublin as a child and I still love this vibrant city. If you like shopping, try Grafton Street, with its buskers and Molly Malone's statue. But also visit Trinity College to see the Book of Kells, take in a play at the Abbey or Gate Theatres, or just enjoy the cobbled streets of the Temple Bar area, abuzz with art studios, shops, cafes and bars.'

POST – CARD

Cefalù in Sicily

Reader Caroline Bullen, from Chichester in West Sussex, nominates the town of Cefalù in Sicily

'I enjoyed a wonderful holiday touring Sicily last year and particularly loved Cefalù, which lies on the northern coast. Despite its tiny size, this fascinating town attracts millions of tourists every year. It has a wonderful sandy beach with colourful boats, and a magnificent Sicilian Romanesque cathedral towering above the streets, with two four-storey towers.'

7 Monday

8 Tuesday

9 Wednesday

10 Thursday

11 Friday

12 Saturday

13 Sunday

Griddled Prawns & Avocado Salad

SERVES *2*
CALORIES *500*
FAT *28g*
SATURATED FAT *5g*
SUITABLE FOR FREEZING *No*

INGREDIENTS

* 100g (3½oz) bulgar wheat
* 4 thin spring onions, trimmed and finely chopped
* 6 Kalamata olives, stoned and chopped
* About 100g (3½oz) Piccolo cherry tomatoes, quartered
* 2 handfuls of fresh flat-leaf parsley leaves
* 1 handful of fresh dill sprigs
* 1-2 tablespoons lemon juice
* 1 small avocado, peeled, stoned and sliced
* 2 tablespoons olive oil
* 150g (5oz) raw prawns
* Salt and ground black pepper

1 Rinse the bulgar wheat. Put it in a bowl and cover with about 100ml (3½fl oz) boiling water and leave for 5-10 minutes.

2 Add the spring onions, olives, tomatoes, herbs, lemon juice, sliced avocado and half the oil. Stir together gently.

3 Coat the prawns in the rest of the oil and cook them for a few minutes on a hot griddle (or hot wok or frying pan) until they turn pink all over.

4 Next, divide the salad between 2 bowls, then top with the prawns and season well.

TIP FROM OUR KITCHEN

Roughly chop the herbs and add some mint leaves for extra freshness.

Your Good Health

Ask Dr Mel

Q I'm due to fly across several times zones soon. What should I do about taking my regular medication?

A Pack all your medication in your hand luggage; keep pills in their original labelled packs to avoid awkward questions. Check with the airline — you may need a doctor's letter confirming that you're prescribed these, or that you need to carry liquid medicines or needles and syringes.

Medicine timing depends on what you're taking, how often, and how long you'll be there. You could stick to UK times for short trips, but for longer ones you'll need to adapt to local time. Adapting might involve shortening or extending the time between doses or missing a dose altogether. With many drugs, you can safely "slide" dose times by a couple of hours each day (although this could mean taking them in the middle of the night). But dose-sliding could be dangerous if you take insulin or drugs for diabetes, medicines that can be toxic when the dose is exceeded, or drugs that stop protecting you if taken late, such as the contraceptive pill. The safest thing is to ask your GP, who can give you specific advice based on your medical conditions and treatment.

TRY THIS Hypnotherapy

When you're trying to lose weight, it's easy to get derailed by food cravings. Hypnotherapy can help change your attitude towards certain foods by releasing the habits associated with them. "A quick visualisation exercise is to imagine the food you crave as a red triangle, then put your feelings about the food in this shape and shrink it down. Repeat until the craving passes," suggests hypnotherapist Ailsa Frank (www.hypnobalance.co.uk).

HEALTH ON MY SHELF

Michelle Berriedale-Johnson, food allergy campaigner

What's in your medicine cabinet?
Tea tree oil; Solpadeine for headaches.

What's good in your fridge?
Lots of fresh veg — leaves, sprouting seeds; fresh green olives; oat milk.

What's your favourite exercise?
I do ten minutes of yoga exercises each morning, followed by running on the spot.

What's a special treat?
Walks on Hampstead Heath and BoojaBooja ice cream (from www.boojabooja.com).

What makes you stressed?
Too much electro-smog (mobile phones, Wi-Fi, etc).

If you can't sleep, what works?
A banana and the World Service.

Any childhood remedy you still use?
A bowl of custard made with a dollop of raspberry jam when I'm feeling off-colour!
Michelle offers advice and support at www. foodsmatter.com; www.coeliacsmatter.com and www.skinsmatter.com

TAKE 6...
Care For Your Mouth

1 KEEP IT WELL-HYDRATED with regular non-sugary drinks and rinse out with water after meals.

2 USE SUGAR-FREE chewing gum to stimulate saliva flow.

3 BRUSH TEETH twice daily using a soft toothbrush and fluoridated toothpaste, then use dental floss.

4 IF YOU WEAR DENTURES, clean them daily and store them in a recommended denture solution at night.

5 DRINK ALCOHOL ONLY within recommended limits, and don't smoke or chew tobacco.

6 IF AN ULCER, sore, swelling, roughened area, or a red/white patch lasts more than three weeks, show your GP or dentist.

14 Monday

15 Tuesday

16 Wednesday

17 Thursday

18 Friday

19 Saturday

20 Sunday

Summer Garland

Celebrate the sunshine with our colourful bunting

MEASUREMENTS
Each triangle measures 17.5cm/7in at base and 20.5cm/8in from base to point.

MATERIALS
2 x 50g balls of Rico Essentials Cotton DK in each of Blue (Light Teal 29), Pink (Fuchsia 14) and Lime (Pistachio 86). One ball in each of Yellow (Banana 63) and Orange (Tangerine 69). Pair of 4mm (No. 8), knitting needles; 5m of 1.5cm wide ribbon. Yarn costs about

£2.50 per 50g ball. For yarn stockists, call 020 3024 9009. The yarn can be purchased from Crafty Yarns (0118 943 1144; www.crafty-yarn.co.uk) or Black Sheep (01925 764231; www.blacksheepwools.co.uk) or Multi-Ply (01723 364191; www.multiplywools.co.uk).

TENSION
21 stitches and 31 rows, to 10 x 10cm, over stocking stitch, using 4mm needles.

ABBREVIATIONS
K, knit; **p,** purl; **st,** stitch; **tog,** together; **p2togb,** p2tog through back of sts; **dec,** decrease (by taking 2 sts tog); **ss,** stocking st (k on right side and p on wrong side); **gst,** garter st (every row k); **skpo,** slip 1, k1, pass slip st over.

NOTE
Yarn amounts are based on average requirements and are therefore approximate.

PLAIN TRIANGLES

With 4mm needles and Pink, cast on 38 sts.
1st row: K. **2nd row:** K3, p to last 3 sts, k3.
Repeat last 2 rows, 5 times more.
1st (dec) row: K3, k2tog, k to last 5 sts, skpo, k3. **2nd row:** K3, p to last 3 sts, k3. **3rd row:** K.
4th (dec) row: K3, p2togb, p to last 5 sts, p2tog, k3. **5th row:** K.
6th row: K3, p to last 3 sts, k3.
Repeat last 6 rows, 6 times more — 10 sts.
Shape end: 1st row: K3, k2tog, skpo, k3 — 8 sts. **2nd row:** K3, p2, k3. **3rd row:** K2, k2tog, skpo, k2 — 6 sts. **4th row:** K6. **5th row:** K1, k2tog, skpo, k1 — 4 sts. **6th row:** K4. **7th row:** K2tog, skpo — 2 sts. **8th row:** K2. **9th row:** K2tog and fasten off.
Make 1 more in each of Yellow, Lime and Orange.

STRIPED TRIANGLES

With 4mm needles and Pink, cast on 38 sts.
1st row: K. **2nd row:** K3, p to last 3 sts, k3.
Repeat last 2 rows, once more.

Change to Yellow and repeat 1st and 2nd rows, twice more. The last 8 rows form stripe pattern. Continue in stripe pattern throughout, work another 4 rows.
1st (dec) row: K3, k2tog, k to last 5 sts, skpo, k3. **2nd row:** K3, p to last 3 sts, k3. **3rd row:** K. **4th (dec) row:** K3, p2togb, p to last 5 sts, p2tog, k3. **5th row:** K. **6th row:** K3, p to last 3 sts, k3.
Repeat last 6 rows, 6 times more — 10 sts.
Shape end: 1st row: K3, k2tog, skpo, k3 — 8 sts. **2nd row:** K3, p2, k3. **3rd row:** K2, k2tog, skpo, k2 — 6 sts. **4th row:** K6. **5th row:** K1, k2tog, skpo, k1 — 4 sts. **6th row:** K4. **7th row:** K2tog, skpo — 2 sts. **8th row:** K2. **9th row:** K2tog and fasten off.
Make 1 more triangle, using Lime instead of Yellow. Make 1 more triangle, using Lime instead of Pink and Blue instead of Yellow. Make 1 more triangle, using Lime instead of Pink and Orange instead of Yellow.

TWO-COLOUR TRIANGLES

With 4mm needles and Pink, cast on 19 sts, join in Lime and cast on 19 more sts.
When changing colours, twist yarns together on wrong sides at

joins to avoid making holes.
1st row: K19 Lime, k19 Pink.
2nd row: With Pink, k3, p16, with Lime p16, k3.
The last 2 rows form pattern. Continue in pattern throughout and work thus: Pattern another 10 rows.
1st (dec) row: K3, k2tog, k to last 5 sts, skpo, k3. **2nd row:** K3, p to last 3 sts, k3. **3rd row:** K.
4th (dec) row: K3, p2togb, p to last 5 sts, p2tog, k3. **5th row:** K.
6th row: K3, p to last 3 sts, k3.
Repeat last 6 rows, 6 times more — 10 sts. **Shape end: 1st row:** K3, k2tog, skpo, k3 — 8 sts. **2nd row:** K3, p2, k3. **3rd row:** K2, k2tog, skpo, k2 — 6 sts. **4th row:** K6. **5th row:** K1, k2tog, skpo, k1 — 4 sts. **6th row:** K4. **7th row:** K2tog, skpo — 2 sts. **8th row:** K2. 9th row: K2tog and fasten off.
Make 1 more triangle, using Orange instead of Pink. Make 1 more triangle, using Yellow instead of Pink and Pink instead of Lime. Make 1 more triangle, using Lime instead of Pink and Yellow instead of Lime.

TRIANGLES WITH SPOTS

(MAKE 5)
With 4mm needles and Blue, cast on 38 sts.

Using separate lengths of yarn for each spot and twisting yarns together on wrong side at joins, continue thus:

1st row: With Blue, k. **2nd row:** With Blue, k3, p11, p2 Lime, with Blue, p19, k3. **3rd row:** K21 Blue, 4 Lime, 13 Blue. **4th row:** With Blue, k3, p10, p4 Lime, p13 Blue, p2 Yellow, with Blue, p3, k3. **5th row:** K5 Blue, 4 Yellow, 12 Blue, 4 Lime, 13 Blue. **6th row:** With Blue, k3, p11, p2 Lime, p13 Blue, p4 Yellow, with Blue, p2, k3. **7th row:** K5 Blue, 4 Yellow, 29 Blue. **8th row:** With Blue, k3, p3, p2 Orange, p12 Blue, p2 Pink, p8 Blue, p2 Yellow, with Blue, p3, k3. **9th row:** K15 Blue, 4 Pink, 10 Blue, 4 Orange, 5 Blue. **10th row:** With Blue, k3, p2, p4 Orange, p10 Blue, p4 Pink, with Blue, p12, k3. **11th row:** K15 Blue, 4 Pink, 10 Blue, 4 Orange, 5 Blue. **12th row:** With Blue, k3, p3, p2 Orange, p12 Blue, p2 Pink, with Blue, p13, k3. **13th row:** With Blue, k3, k2tog, k3, k2 Lime, k13 Blue, k2 Yellow, with Blue, k8, skpo, k3. **14th row:** With Blue, k3, p8, p4 Yellow, p11 Blue, p4 Lime, with Blue, p3, k3. **15th row:** K6 Blue, 4 Lime, 11 Blue, 4 Yellow, 11 Blue. **16th row:** With Blue, k3, p2togb, p6, p4 Yellow, p11 Blue, p4 Lime, with Blue, p1, p2tog, k3. **17th row:** K6 Blue, 2 Lime, 13 Blue, 2 Yellow, 11 Blue. **18th row:** With Blue, k3, p17, p2 Orange, with Blue, p9, k3. **19th row:** With Blue, k3, k2tog, k6, k4 Orange, k10 Blue, k2 Pink, with Blue, k2, skpo, k3. **20th row:** With Blue, k3, p2, p4 Pink, p9 Blue, p4 Orange, with Blue, p7, k3. **21st row:** K10 Blue, 4 Orange, 9 Blue, 4 Pink, 5 Blue. **22nd row:** With Blue, k3, p2togb, p4 Pink, p10 Blue, p2 Orange, with Blue, p6, p2tog, k3. **23rd row:** K16 Blue, 2 Lime, 5 Blue, 2 Pink, 5 Blue. **24th row:** With Blue, k3, p8, p4 Lime, with Blue, p12, k3. **25th row:** With Blue, k3, k2tog, k10, k4 Lime, with Blue, k6, skpo, k3. **26th row:** With Blue, k3, p7, p4 Lime, with Blue, p11, k3. **27th row:** K6 Blue, 2 Yellow, 7 Blue, 2 Lime, 11 Blue. **28th row:** With Blue, k3, p2togb, p14, p4 Yellow, with Blue, p2tog, k3. **29th row:** K4 Blue, 4 Yellow,

Each pennant of this cheery bunting is knitted in stocking-stitch with garter-stitch edgings in a variety of patterns. The yarn is pure cotton.

18 Blue. **30th row:** With Blue, k3, p3, p2 Orange, p10 Blue, p4 Yellow, with Blue, p1, k3. **31st row:** With Blue, k3, k2tog, k2 Yellow, k10 Blue, k4 Orange, with Blue, skpo, k3. **32nd row:** With Blue, k3, p1, p4 Orange, with Blue, p13, k3. **33rd row:** K16 Blue, 4 Orange, 4 Blue. **34th row:** With Blue, k3, p2togb, p2 Orange, p6 Blue, p2 Pink, with Blue, p4, p2tog, k3. **35th row:** K7 Blue, 4 Pink, 11 Blue. **36th row:** With Blue, k3, p8, p4 Pink, with Blue, p4, k3. **37th row:** With Blue, k3, k2tog, k2, k4 Pink, with Blue, k6, skpo, k3. **38th row:** With Blue, k3, p8, p2 Pink, with Blue, p4, k3. **39th row:** K12 Blue, 2 Lime, 6 Blue. **40th row:** With Blue, k3, p2togb, p4 Lime, with Blue, p6, p2tog, k3. **41st row:** K10 Blue, 4 Lime, 4 Blue. **42nd row:** With Blue, k3, p1, p4 Lime, with Blue, p7, k3. **43rd row:** With Blue, k3, k2tog, k6, k2 Lime, with Blue, skpo, k3. **44th row:** With

Blue, k3, p10, k3. **45th row:** K6 Blue, 2 Yellow, 8 Blue. **46th row:** With Blue, k3, p2togb, p2, p4 Yellow, with Blue, p2tog, k3. **47th row:** K4 Blue, 4 Yellow, 6 Blue. **48th row:** With Blue, k3, p3, p4 Yellow, with Blue, p1, k3. **49th row:** With Blue, k3, k2tog, k2 Yellow, with Blue, k2, skpo, k3. Continue in Blue only. **50th row:** K3, p6, k3. **51st row:** K. **52nd row:** K3, p2togb, p2, p2tog, k3. **53rd row:** K. **54th row:** K3, p4, k3. **55th row:** K3, k2tog, skpo, k3. **56th row:** K3, p2, k3. **57th row:** K2, k2tog, skpo, k2 — 6 sts. **58th row:** K6. **59th row:** K1, k2tog, skpo, k1 — 4 sts. **60th row:** K4. **61st row:** K2tog, skpo — 2 sts. **62nd row:** K2. **63rd row:** K2tog and fasten off.

TO MAKE UP

Leaving 6cm gaps between each triangle, sew cast-on edge of triangles to ribbon, in desired order.

Karen Has News

She wanted to remember this moment forever. It was the beginning of a whole new chapter in her life

Karen stepped outside the surgery and realised just how beautiful Marsh Road actually was.

OK, so there was the bus stop with the cracked pane of glass and the graffiti. And workmen were digging up the pavement a few yards away and the reek of hot tar clogged the air. It was overcast too and threatening rain.

But despite all that, it was still beautiful. Because today was the day Doctor McGiven said, "Congratulations, Karen."

This was the beginning of a whole new chapter in her life. The start of something fresh. The dawn of a new day. She wanted to remember this moment forever.

She wanted to run yelling down the road, shout her news from the rooftops, accost total strangers. But she didn't, of course. Because she was Karen Langdale and Karen Langdale didn't do things like that. Although maybe the old Karen didn't. Who could tell what the new one might do?

She surreptitiously clenched a fist and let out a whispered, "Wahey".

She'd taken the bus to get there. It was a good three miles from home to the surgery. But now she didn't care about becoming all hot and sweaty, so she set off walking, swinging her handbag jauntily.

Nothing was going to spoil her day.

"Woo-hoo!" called a voice from across the road. "Ka-ren!"

Not even Angie Pettifer, who was on the other side of the crossing.

Karen quickly wondered whether she could get away with trying to ignore her nemesis. But it was too late now. Be rude not to at least say hello.

"Hello, Angie," she said.

"Long time, no speak," Angie said. 'Thank goodness', Karen silently added.

Angie was dressed in the tightest jeans available to modern science and was wearing a low-cut top that appeared to have two bald men hiding unsuccessfully inside it.

"So, how are you doing then, Karen?" Angie asked.

"Actually, I've just come from the doh..." No! She didn't want Angie Pettifer to be the first to hear her news. "...doh-nut shop," she finished.

"Hmm, doesn't surprise me." Angie arched a perfectly-manicured eyebrow and glanced at Karen's belly. "Been there a lot lately, by the looks of it."

"I beg your..! Actually, I'm..." 'No, don't get drawn in,' she told herself. 'It's a good day today. Not a bad one. Focus.'

"You've always been fond of your food, haven't you? I remember at school. Always first in the queue at the tuck shop."

Why did Angie have to say these things? Every time, too? Lies! They didn't have a queue for the tuck shop at school. It was more of a free-for-all. Karen had merely been good with her elbows.

"Sorry, Angie, I'd love to chat —" No, she wouldn't — "but I have to be somewhere—" No, she didn't — "and I should be getting along."

"Which way are you going? I'll walk with you."

"That way."

"Same as me."

"I meant that way."

"Oh." Angie rallied quickly. "I will say, though, you look very, how shall I put it? Very... healthy. Radiant, in fact." Angie seemed surprised by this.

Karen grinned. "Can't think why! Anyway, must dash. 'Bye!"

"'Bye then," Angie replied, but Karen was already off and away.

'Just goes to show,' Karen thought. On a day like today, not even Angie Pettifer's barbed comments could make a dent in her good mood.

Oh, it was no good! She simply had to tell Mark her news right now. She couldn't keep it in any longer. She pulled out her mobile phone.

'But hold on,' she thought, as her thumb hovered over speed-dial, 'what if he's busy? He might be with people. Might not want to speak about personal matters.' And besides, she really did want to break the news in person, where they could hug and kiss and she could see his reaction.

No, better to do the big announcement at home. After all the sleepless nights and the worrying it might never happen, it was silly to rush the announcement now.

So, a few hours later, Mark rolled in from work, loosening his tie and throwing down his briefcase.

"I have news," Karen blurted out, cracking the moment she saw him. "Big news."

"News?" Mark frowned.

"Things are going to be different from now on. Very different."

"You don't mean..?"

She nodded excitedly. "I do! I was at the surgery today. Saw Doctor McGiven." She'd been trying for so, so long that she thought it might never happen. "You're now looking at his new receptionist!"

A new job, at last! Almost as good as when she found out she was expecting Mark...

THE END
© Steve Beresford

> *Oh, it was no good! She simply had to tell him her news right now*

21 Monday

22 Tuesday

23 Wednesday

24 Thursday

25 Friday

26 Saturday

27 Sunday

In The Frame

Turn an everyday item into something completely different

Take a picture frame — and transform it into a unique and original gift that can be assembled in moments, using only the most basic sewing and crafting skills. All you need is a little imagination and three easy steps to create our stunning jewellery stand.

From picture frame to jewellery stand

1 Remove the glass and backing board from your chosen frame. Cut a piece of stiff card to the same size as the backing board. For the background, cut a piece of pretty patterned wrapping paper or fabric to fit the card, allowing 2cm extra all around. Cover the card with the paper or fabric, folding the excess to the wrong side; neaten the corners to reduce bulk and hold in place with sticky tape.

2 Using the picture as a guide, cut a selection of ribbons, braids and lace trimmings to fit across the width of the covered background, adding an extra 3cm. Arrange the trimmings in horizontal lines across the background, folding the excess at each end around the back. Once you're happy with the arrangement, secure the ends in place with a staple, making sure they're not visible from the front when the frame is in place.

3 Place the decorated card, followed by the backing board, in the frame. Use the strips of ribbon and trimmings to display your jewellery, either hanging, clipping or pinning individual pieces in place.

Rococo-style picture frame, £25, Marks & Spencer (0845 302 1234; www. marksandspencer.com); wrapping paper, £2 per sheet, Paperchase (020 7467 6200; www.paperchase.co.uk); vintage ribbons, similar available from John Lewis (0845 604 9049; www.johnlewis.com); diamanté bird hair clip, £15, diamanté star brooch, £18, rose hair clips, £6, flower earrings, £5, vintage lace flower necklace, £70, pearl bracelet with bird charm, £40, all from Attic (020 8943 9626; www.discoverattic.com).

28 Monday

29 Tuesday

30 Wednesday

31 Thursday

1 Friday

2 Saturday

3 Sunday

CROSSWORD

Read down the letters
in the shaded squares to
spell out a craftsman (9)

ACROSS

12 Accident victims (10)
13 Soft drinks and light snacks (12)
14 Hour of the day (6)
15 Dawdlers (9)
16 Worker who collects rubbish (6)
17 Long adventure film (4)
19 The Pink ___, cartoon
character (7)
21 Symbol representing the US
currency unit (6,4)
23 Except if (6)
24 Deserted, forsaken (9)
26 Upright part of a staircase
between treads (5)
27 TV series aboard the
Enterprise (4,4)
29 Swiss ___, cylindrical
sponge cake (4)
30 Prepare (to do) (4,5)
32 Small roofed stall for the sale of
sweets, papers etc (5)
34 Remove clothes (5)
36 Zany, madcap (5)
37 Thin length of leather (5)
41 Physical attractiveness (3,6)
42 ___ Banks, model and actress (4)
43 Whinnying (8)
46 Float aimlessly (5)
47 In good supply (9)
48 Reroute or amuse (6)
50 Iron, copper etc with a thickness
between foil and plate (5,5)
53 Use up (7)
55 Pleasant, enjoyable (4)
56 ___ Ransome, Swallows and
Amazons author (6)
58 Annoys (9)
60 Draw back in horror (6)
62 Refusal to follow commands (12)
63 Animal with a backbone (10)

DOWN

1 Pot used for cooking (8)
2 Martial art form (4)
3 Thin-layered piecrust (5,6)
4 Instrument played with a bow (6)
5 Perfectly fit and well (2,5,2,4)
6 At liberty (4)
7 Committing crime (9)
8 Ship or container (6)
9 Unreasonable fear (6)
10 Keep on a tight ___, strictly
control (4)
11 Giving each other filthy
looks (2,7,5)
18 Shout 'hurrah' (5)
20 Puzzling question (6)
22 Person believed to be guilty (7)
24 Noah's boat (3)
25 Swallowed liquid (5)
26 Length of film (4)

28 Person behind others in
a group (4-3,7)
31 Primus, eg (8,5)
33 Place with a beach (7)
35 Homeless wanderer (5)
38 Argument (4)
39 Supernatural (6)
40 Generous, warm and
friendly (4-7)
43 Score of nothing in sport (3)
44 Shelter, safe place (5)
45 Proclaiming (9)
49 Proofs of payment (8)
51 Town's open-air trading place (6)
52 Petty or useless information (6)
54 Not certain (6)
57 Cry of an owl (4)
59 Person older than twelve but
younger than twenty (4)
61 Restore to health (4)

Solutions to this month's puzzle on next month's puzzle

SOLUTIONS FOR JUNE, 2014

NOTEPAD

SINGING

AUGUST

Time To Shine

Shimmer your way from day to night and complete your summer look with this simple satin bolero

MEASUREMENTS

To fit sizes 81-86 (91) (97) (102) (107) cm/32-34 (36) (38) (40) (42) in.
Actual measurements, all round at underarms 91 (97) (103) (109) (115) cm/36 (38) (40½) (42¾) (45¼) in.
Side seam, including edging 19 (19.5) (20) (21) (22) cm/7½ (7¾) (8) (8¼) (8½) in.
Length to shoulder, including edging 37 (37.5) (39) (41.5) (43.5) cm/14½ (14¾) (15¼) (16¼) (17) in.
Sleeve seam, including edging 9cm/3½in.

MATERIALS

Pair of 4mm (No. 8) and 5½mm (No. 5) knitting needles. A 4mm (No. 8) circular knitting needle. 1 x 450g cone of Yeoman Tian (100-per-cent nylon). Yarn is available by mail order only and costs £15.95 per 450g cone, including p&p. We used Silver (21), but there are other shades available. For more yarn details, write to Yeoman Yarns Ltd, 36 Churchill Way, Fleckney, Leics LE8 8UD, call 0116 240 4464, email sales@yeomanyarns.co.uk or visit www.yeoman-yarns.co.uk.

TENSION

20 stitches and 26 rows, to 10 x 10cm, over stocking stitch, using 5½mm needles.

ABBREVIATIONS

K, knit; **p,** purl; **st,** stitch; **ss,** stocking st (k on right side and p on wrong side); **tog,** together; **inc,** increase (by working twice into same st); **up1,** pick up loop lying between needles and work into back of it; **nil,** meaning nothing is worked here for this size; **skpo,** slip1, k1, pass slip st over; **yrn,** yarn round needle to make a st.

NOTE

Yarn amounts quoted are based on average requirements and are therefore approximate. Instructions are given for small size. Where they vary, work figures in round brackets for larger sizes. Instructions in square brackets are worked as stated after 2nd bracket.

MAIN PART

Back: With 5½mm needles, cast on 74 (80) (86) (92) (98) sts. Beginning with a k row, ss 4 (6) (8) (10) (12) rows.
Shape sides: Increase row: K2, up1, k to last 2 sts, up1, k2. Beginning with a p row, ss 5 rows. Repeat last 6 rows, 4 times more — 84 (90) (96) (102) (108) sts.
Shape underarms: Increase row: K2, up1, k to last 2 sts, up1, k2.
Next row: P.
Repeat last 2 rows, 4 times more — 94 (100) (106) (112) (118) sts.
Shape for sleeves: Continuing in ss, cast on 14 sts at beginning of next 2 rows — 122 (128) (134) (140) (146) sts.
Ss 37 (37) (39) (41) (43) rows.

Dividing row: P46 (49) (51) (53) (55) and leave these sts on a spare needle for shoulder and left front, cast off next 30 (30) (32) (34) (36) sts for centre back neck, p to end and work on remaining 46 (49) (51) (53) (55) sts for shoulder and right front.

Shoulder and right front: Ss 8 (8) (8) (10) (12) rows, marking each end of 7th (7th) (7th) (9th) (10th) of these rows for shoulder.
Inc 1 st at end — neck edge — of next row and 7 (7) (6) (6) (5) following 6th rows and nil (nil) (2) (3) (5) following 4th rows — 54 (57) (60) (63) (66) sts.
P1 row.
Shape for sleeve: Cast off 14 sts at beginning of next row — 40 (43) (46) (49) (52) sts.
Next row: P.

Shape underarms: Next row: K2, skpo, k to end.
Next row: P.
Repeat last 2 rows, 3 times more — 36 (39) (42) (45) (48) sts.
Shape side: Next row: K2, skpo, k to end.
Beginning with a p row, ss 5 rows.
Repeat last 6 rows, once more — 34 (37) (40) (43) (46) sts.
Shape front edge and continue to shape side: Next row: K2, skpo, k to last 2 sts, k2tog.
Next row: P.
Next row: K to last 2 sts, k2tog.
Next row: P
Next row: K to last 2 sts, k2tog.
Next row: P.
Repeat last 6 rows, twice more, then work the 1st of these rows again — 20 (23) (26) (29) (32) sts.
Keeping side edge straight,

Next row: Skpo, k to end.
Next row: P.
Next row: Skpo, k to end.
Next row: P.
Repeat last 6 rows, twice more, then work 1st of these rows again — 20 (23) (26) (29) (32) sts. Keeping side edge straight, dec 1 st at front edge on next 5 (7) (9) (11) (13) rows — 15 (16) (17) (18) (19) sts.
Cast off.

SLEEVE EDGINGS
(BOTH ALIKE)
With right side facing, using 4mm needles, pick up and k79 (79) (85) (91) (97) sts evenly along row-ends of sleeve. K 4 rows.
Next row (wrong side): [P2tog, yrn] to last st, p1.
K 3 rows. Cast off kwise.

LOWER AND FRONT EDGING
Join side and sleeve seams. With right side facing, beginning at lower edge at left side seam and using 4mm circular needle, pick up and k101 (107) (113) (119) (125) sts evenly along cast-on edge of back, 21 (22) (23) (24) (25) sts along cast-off edge of right front, 28 (30) (32) (34) (36) sts around curve, 76 (76) (80) (82) (85) sts up right front edge to back neck, 38 (38) (40) (42) (44) sts across cast-off sts at centre back neck, 76 (76) (80) (82) (85) sts down left front edge to curve, 28 (30) (32) (34) (36) around curve, and finally, 21 (22) (23) (24) (25) sts along cast-off edge of left front — 389 (401) (423) (441) (461) sts. Working backwards and forwards in rows, work edging as given for sleeve edgings.

TO MAKE UP
Join row-ends of edging at left side. Sew in ends, knotting ends of yarn to stop yarn unravelling.

dec 1 st at front edge on next 5 (7) (9) (11) (13) rows — 15 (16) (17) (18) (19) sts.
Cast off.
With right side facing, rejoin yarn to inner edge of 46 (49) (51) (53) (55) sts on spare needle, k to end and work on these sts for shoulder and left front
Shoulder and left front: Ss 7 (7) (7) (9) (11) rows, marking each end of 6th (6th) (6th) (8th) (9th) of these rows for shoulder.
Inc 1 st at beginning — neck edge — of next row and 7 (7) (6) (6) (5) following 6th rows and nil (nil) (2) (3) (5) following 4th rows — 54 (57) (60) (63) (66) sts.

Ss 2 rows.
Shape for sleeve: Cast off 14 sts at beginning of next row — 40 (43) (46) (49) (52) sts.
Shape underarms: Next row: K to last 4 sts, k2tog, k2.
Next row: P.
Repeat last 2 rows, 3 times more — 36 (39) (42) (45) (48) sts.
Shape side: Next row: K to last 4 sts, k2tog, k2.
Beginning with a p row, ss 5 rows.
Repeat last 6 rows, once more — 34 (37) (40) (43) (46) sts.
Shape front edge and continue to shape side: Next row: Skpo, k to last 4 sts, k2tog, k2.
Next row: P.

Your Good Health

Ask Dr Mel

Q I am experiencing repeated attacks of cystitis. How can I avoid it?

A Cystitis means bladder irritation, and is often due to urine infections. It produces a frequent or urgent need to urinate, day and/or night, with burning and irritation in the urethra (the pipe that empties the bladder) and/or low tummy pain. Your urine may smell unpleasant or look cloudy/bloodstained; cystitis can also lead to kidney infections, with fever, vomiting and back pain. But vaginal thrush, dryness due to oestrogen deficiency, and narrowing of the urethra (stricture), can also produce similar symptoms, while blood in the urine, or recurrent cystitis may be due to bladder inflammation or even cancer. So it's important to have your urine checked when you get cystitis, and you may need tests, such as an ultrasound scan and a cystoscopy (telescope examination of the bladder).

But if it's straightforward cystitis, there's lots you can do to help yourself. Drink plenty of fluid (including a daily glass of cranberry juice). Empty your bladder regularly, wiping front to back. Washing before intercourse, and urinating before and afterwards, can prevent honeymoon-type cystitis; a single dose of antibiotic beforehand, or regular use of oestrogen vaginal cream, may also help.

TRY THIS) Eye Exercises

"Exercises can help strengthen and stretch eye muscles just as a gym workout keeps your body in shape," says Karen Sparrow, adviser at the Association of Optometrists. Try this: Squeeze your eyes tight shut and hold for three seconds. Let go and open your eyes as wide as you can. Hold for three seconds. Repeat five times. With your head still, look up and hold for five seconds. Cast eyes down and hold for five seconds. Move eyes left, then right, holding for five seconds. Look across up to the left and down to the right. Hold for five seconds each time.

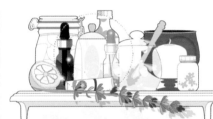

HEALTH ON MY SHELF
Kathryn Colas, menopause expert

What's in your medicine cabinet?
Electric Body face cream. And Solgar Omega 3-6-9 — it oils the parts other supplements cannot reach.

What's good in your fridge?
Lemons. One of my favourite drinks is hot water, lemon and a teaspoon of honey.

What's your favourite exercise?
I do 10 minutes of stretches each morning, including sit-ups, the plank, and star jumps.

If you can't sleep, what works?
Meditation — it used to sound airy fairy to me until I learned how to do it.

What's a special healthy treat?
A bowl of berries with a couple of dollops of plain yogurt and a teaspoon of honey.

What makes you happy?
My granddaughter! She's an absolute joy.

Any childhood remedy you still use?
Warmed almond or olive oil for earache.
Kathryn Colas is the creator of www. simplyhormones.com and www. mentoringthroughmenopause.com.

TAKE 5...
Relieve Varicose Veins

1 IMPROVE THE CONDITION of your skin by moisturising legs daily.

2 KEEP YOUR WEIGHT DOWN to relieve aching, prevent further varicose veins and reduce complications.

3 AVOID PROLONGED STANDING; keep the muscle pump working by pulling up your toes, standing up (and down) on your toes or doing kneebends. Exercise regularly.

4 PUT YOUR FEET UP whenever you sit down to improve blood flow.

5 WEAR SUPPORT TIGHTS to exert "inward" pressure on vein walls. Your GP can prescribe stronger compression stockings.

4 Monday

5 Tuesday

6 Wednesday

7 Thursday

8 Friday

9 Saturday

10 Sunday

Have a go at..
Perfume-Making

You can create your own special scent with our step-by-step guide

Using a combination of essential and fragrance oils, we've created a perfume — *Woman's Weekly* Summer Bouquet. You can make your own version, too, testing out different blends on cotton wool. Your scent is ready for use immediately, and will have a shelf life of two to three years.

YOU WILL NEED

* Five different essential or fragrance oils, to create your unique perfume blends
* Cotton-wool pads, to use as smelling pads
* Perfumer's alcohol, to dilute your perfume
* Measuring beaker
* Smelling sticks, to test your perfume
* Perfume bottle

PERFUME POINTERS

Before using any of the products you make, carry out a patch test. Place a little of the product on the skin of your inner arm. If, after 24 hours, there's no redness, itchiness or adverse reaction to the product, it's fine to use. Your perfumes should be for personal use only and can't be sold commercially, unless your product formulation has been certified by a cosmetic chemist.

1 BLENDING ON COTTON WOOL
Place drops of different essential or fragrance oils on a cotton-wool pad to experience how they smell together. For example, add one drop each of rose, lemon and vanilla. Ensure that the drops are on top of each other on the cotton-wool pad, so they blend together properly. Wave the pad gently in the air in front of your nose and then smell the aroma. Adjust by adding another drop as necessary.

2 BLENDING
When creating your scent, try to use at least four different essential or fragrance oils. Many shop-bought perfumes are made from more than 25 individual scents. The blends that you create

don't need to have equal amounts of your chosen oils. For our blend, we used two drops of lemon, two drops of lily of the valley, three drops of rose, two drops of tea rose and one drop of vanilla. Once you've decided on your blend, you need about 60 drops altogether to make a subtle daytime perfume. In our example above, we used ten drops in total. Ten divided into 60 equals six, so we multiplied each drop of oil we used by six, making the final formula 12 drops of lemon, 12 drops of lily of the valley, 18 drops of rose, 12 drops of tea rose and six drops of vanilla. For a stronger, longer-lasting aroma, you can put in up to double the amount of perfume blend (120 drops) with 25ml perfumer's alcohol.

3 MAKING THE PERFUME
Once you've decided what blend you're going to create, carefully place the 60 or so drops of your chosen fragrance or essential oils into a measuring beaker. Then top up with approximately 25ml of perfumer's alcohol. Stir with a smelling stick. Then pour into your perfume bottle.

TIP
If you attach the cotton-wool pad to a piece of paper and then add the oils, you can write down which ones you've used — just in case you forget!

Mudford Beach in Dorset

POST – CARD

Reader Janet Ladhams, from Abertillery, Gwent, recommends Mudeford Beach, near Christchurch, in Dorset

'I visit Mudeford whenever I can, because it never fails to lift my mood. The beach has a wildness about it. I love to walk along the shoreline after a storm to see what's been washed up. Off shore, cormorants dive for fish, and in the distance you can see the Needles off the Isle of Wight. It's perfect for reflection, away from the business of everyday life — and is my sanctuary.'

Cape Peninsula in South Africa

POST – CARD

Reader Deryn van der Tang, from Bedford, nominates the Cape Peninsula in South Africa

'Sir Francis Drake called it "The fairest cape in all the world". I love to climb the Tygerberg Hills, with their 360-degree view, and look out across Table Bay to the mountain and to Robben Island. Looking in another direction, the Hottentots-Holland Mountains, with their jagged tops, cut the skyline and below them lie the vineyards. There is so much to see and do; the world in one place.'

11 Monday
_____

12 Tuesday
_____

13 Wednesday
_____

14 Thursday
_____

15 Friday
_____

16 Saturday
_____

17 Sunday
_____

Tomato & Pepper Galettes

SERVES 4
CALORIES 371
FAT 25g
SATURATED FAT 8g
SUITABLE FOR FREEZING No

INGREDIENTS

* 2 peppers, yellow and orange, deseeded and cut into thick strips
* 1 onion, peeled and cut into thin wedges
* 3 sprigs of thyme
* 3 tablespoons olive oil
* 250g (8oz) all-butter puff pastry (half a 500g pack)
* 2 tablespoons chopped fresh parsley
* 12 kalamata olives, pitted
* 16-20 baby plum tomatoes, halved
* Salt and ground black pepper
* Baking sheet, lightly buttered

1 Set the oven to 190°C or Gas Mark 5. Mix the pepper strips and onion wedges on a baking sheet with thyme sprigs and 2 tablespoons oil. Roast for 30 minutes, stirring occasionally, until they're softened.

2 Meanwhile, roll out the pastry to a square, about 28cm (11in). Cut into 4 x 14cm (5½in) squares. Put them on the baking sheet. Mark a thin border around each one. Prick inside with a fork. Chill for about 30 minutes.

3 Raise the oven temperature to 220°C or Gas Mark 7. Spoon the pepper mixture inside the pastry border. Sprinkle with parsley and add the olives and halved tomatoes. Drizzle with the rest of the oil.

4 Bake for 25 minutes, below the centre of the oven. Season and drizzle with more oil, if you like.

TIP FROM OUR KITCHEN

To make these speedier, you could use roasted red peppers from a jar and to keep them colourful, use multi-coloured cherry tomatoes.

Pluto

She loved those kids like they were her own. But she wasn't their mum. They didn't need her. She was only a temp...

"And then there's Pluto," said Tim, "which has been sort of, like, cast out." Tim was twelve and massively into astronomy. "It's actually not classed as a planet any more." He was giving Sarah a rundown of his latest school science project. "It's been made the head of a new group of solar system objects called Plutoids."

"Plutoids." Sarah nodded. "Sounds like some hideous medical complaint."

Tim laughed and was about to continue when Doug returned with Tim's brother, Nigel, who'd been to the dentist. Nigel was fourteen. Doug was their dad. Neither one looked like him at all. They took after their mum, a woman Sarah had never met.

"How'd it go, Nige?" Sarah asked.

Nigel rocked a hand. "So-so," he replied. He'd made his own way from school to the dentist and Doug had picked him up afterwards. Sarah hadn't seen either of them since breakfast.

"Right, bedrooms, you two," Doug said, waving them away. "Sarah and I need to have a talk."

'Oh, heck,' Sarah thought.

The boys protested, but eventually Doug ushered them away. He had a daughter too — a nineteen-year-old willowy student-slash-trainee journalist. But she was out somewhere. Sarah, at twenty-nine, fell halfway in age between Doug and his daughter.

Doug waited until he heard all the bedroom doors shut. Then he closed the door of the lounge. "It's about what we've been discussing," he said.

"So it's over then?" Sarah glared at him.

"It is for the best. We can't go on. I have the kids to think about. You don't have the same responsibilities."

Which was a nice jab to the ribs. 'Hey, you're not their mum. They don't

need you. You temp!' But she loved those kids like they were her own. "So it's four years down the drain," she said.

"We've had some good times." He frowned. "Haven't we?"

They'd had some wonderful times. Together, as a family. Her friends had warned her about getting involved with a widower who had three children. Nothing but trouble, they all said. Except it hadn't been. Until now.

"There's someone else, isn't there?" Sarah blurted out.

"What? No!" He looked shocked. "I'm ten years older than you, Sarah. I've started to look at you and then I look at Janie, and you two seem more like sisters than my daughter and my partner."

At which point Janie burst into the room. "Oh, Dad!"

"Janie, I didn't know you were back. Have you been eavesdrop—"

"You idiot!" she snapped. Then she threw her arms around Sarah. "I really thought you two would get married," she sobbed on to Sarah's shoulder.

It all got quite emotional after that. The boys came down and they

Sarah cried herself to sleep on her first night alone

were crying too. Sarah cried a lot. Doug, however, remained stony-faced throughout. And that evening Sarah packed her stuff and went to her parents' house. They had a spare room. Sarah had been renting before she moved in with Doug and she could rent again. No biggie, as Janie often said when minor problems came her way. And with that thought of Janie, Sarah cried herself to sleep on her first night alone.

The next week passed by in a blur. Doug phoned her a couple of times, apologising, but adamant he was doing

the right thing. Then, the following Saturday, Doug's children turned up on her parents' doorstep. Janie's rust-bucket was parked behind them.

"Hi, Sarah," said Janie.

"Hello," said Nigel.

"Greetings," said Tim, the space-y one, doing the Vulcan hand symbol thing.

"Dad doesn't know we're here," Janie explained.

"But we wanted to come," Nigel said.

"We've missed you," Tim said.

"And I've missed you," Sarah told them tearfully. She hugged them all as they came in. Then astronomer Tim gave her his theory on the break-up and her place in it.

"We're like the solar system," he said. "And you're like Pluto. You got discovered and became part of our family."

"Then," Janie butted in, "somebody decided you didn't quite fit — namely Dad — and you got booted out."

"So you're a Plutoid," Tim carried on. "No longer actually one of us planets, but you're still there regardless, just like Pluto is."

"He worked all this out himself," Nigel explained.

"Basically—" Janie rolled her eyes — "he's trying to say that Dad might have dumped you, but we haven't. We know it's going to get complicated, but we don't want to have to forget about you just because Dad wants to."

She was right — it would be complicated. But Janie had become more than simply a potential stepdaughter, a child of the man she had once loved. She was also a friend.

"I'll be your Pluto," Sarah managed to say, laughing and crying as the three of them hugged her again, "for as long you want me in orbit."

THE END
© Steve Beresford

18 Monday

19 Tuesday

20 Wednesday

21 Thursday

22 Friday

23 Saturday

24 Sunday

ARROWORD

Clues (reading across the grid):

- Morally bad
- Shopping container (7,3)
- — Healy, Irish singer/songwriter
- Slimy pond organisms
- Boss, familiarly (3,3)
- Sailing boat
- Travel on snow
- Flocks
- Walter de la —, English poet
- Suito[r]
- By way of
- Western defence group (inits)
- Mortified
- Hazy shape
- Actually existing
- Purse (the lips)
- Pole used to row a boat
- Touchdo[wn] in rugb[y]
- — to a Nightingale, Keats poem
- Act of —, catastrophic event
- Lease (4,3)
- Used a keyboard
- Early life
- Very small amount
- — for, pick
- Unable to cope (2,3)
- Faith
- Parents' sisters
- Chums
- Toy on a string (2-2)
- Religious faction
- (Lead) into trouble
- Part of a light
- Salesperson
- Permit, allow
- Relaxed in a chair
- Saucepan
- Eggs of fish
- Fix in a positio[n]
- You'll Never Walk —, song
- Snubs
- Make a noise like an engine
- Back street
- Fence preservative
- Strong, dark, malty ale
- State in court

KRISS KROSS

SECURITY
RAILWAY
AIR
SAFE
SOUP

STITCH
EDGE
TRAIN
FIT
UNIT

Solutions to this month's puzzle on next month's puzzle

SOLUTIONS JULY, 2014

ACROSS: 12 Casualties **13** Refreshments **14** O'clock **15** Loiterers **16** Binman **17** Epic **19** Panther **21** Dollar sign **23** Unless **24** Abandoned **26** Riser **27** Star Trek **29** Roll **30** Make ready **32** Kiosk **34** Strip **36** Wacky **37** Strap **41** Sex appeal **42** Tyra **43** Neighing **46** Drift **47** Plentiful **48** Divert **50** Sheet metal **53** Consume **55** Nice **56** Arthur **58** Irritates **60** Recoil **62** Disobedience **63** Vertebrate
DOWN: 1 Saucepan **2** Judo **3** Flaky pastry **4** Violin **5** As right as rain **6** Free **7** Offending **8** Vessel **9** Phobia **10** Rein **11** At daggers drawn **18** Cheer **20** Riddle **22** Suspect **24** Ark **25** Drank **26** Reel **28** Tail-end charlie **31** Paraffin stove **33** Seaside **35** Tramp **38** Spat **39** Mystic **40** Kind-hearted **43** Nil **44** Haven **45** Declaring **49** Receipts **51** Market **52** Trivia **54** Unsure **57** Hoot **59** Teen **61** Cure
CARPENTER

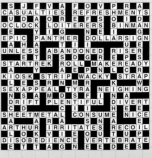

25 Monday SUMMER BANK HOLIDAY

26 Tuesday

27 Wednesday

28 Thursday

29 Friday

30 Saturday

31 Sunday

SEPTEMBER

1 Monday

2 Tuesday

3 Wednesday

4 Thursday

5 Friday

6 Saturday

7 Sunday

Mixed Berry Crisp

SERVES *4*
CALORIES *370*
FAT *14g*
SATURATED FAT *8g*
SUITABLE FOR FREEZING *No*

INGREDIENTS

* *400g pack frozen berries: raspberries, redcurrants, blackcurrants, blackberries (there's no need to defrost them)*
* *4 teaspoons cassis (blackcurrant liqueur), optional*
* *4 teaspoons golden caster sugar*
* *2 level tablespoons thickening granules*

FOR THE TOPPING

* *60g (2oz) butter*
* *60g (2oz) light muscovado sugar*
* *60g (2oz) plain flour*
* *60g (2oz) jumbo oats*
* *½ level teaspoon ground cinnamon*
* *4 teacups, buttered, on a baking tray*

1 Set the oven to 200°C or Gas Mark 6. Divide the frozen berries between the 4 cups. Spoon in the cassis, if using, and sprinkle with the sugar and thickening granules.

2 **To make the topping:** Put the butter and sugar into a pan and heat gently, stirring, to melt the butter and dissolve the sugar. Spoon in the flour, oats and cinnamon.

3 Spoon this flapjack-style topping over the fruit. Bake for 25-30 minutes until topping is golden.

TIP FROM OUR KITCHEN
If you don't want to add the cassis, add an extra teaspoon of sugar to the fruit. You don't need to add any liquid.

POST – CARD

Reader Gillian McDonald from Winlaton, Tyne and Wear, nominates Gosau, in Austria

Gosau in Austria

'On a recent visit to Austria, I fell in love with the dramatic views of the Gosausee, a lake at picturesque Gosau. The reflections took my breath away. At the end of the lake, there is a brilliant view of the Dachstein Massif, the second-highest mountain in the Northern Limestone Alps. This photo, taken by my husband, captures the scenery in all its glory.'

POST – CARD

Reader Rita Collins, from Midleton (chk) in County Cork, chooses the village of Esholt, in West Yorkshire

THE WOOLPACK

Esholt in West Yorkshire

'I am a big fan of *Emmerdale*, so imagine my surprise when I visited my daughter in Liverpool for my birthday last year, and she had arranged a trip to Esholt and its pub, The Woolpack [from 1976 to 1996, Esholt was used for all *Emmerdale*'s outside location shots, now filmed on a purpose-built set]. What beautiful countryside — my best birthday present ever!'

8 Monday

9 Tuesday

10 Wednesday

11 Thursday

12 Friday

13 Saturday

14 Sunday

Just The Jacket

Our no-fuss jacket ticks all the boxes: ☑ Simple, relaxed style
☑ Wear throughout the year
☑ Great wardrobe basic

MEASUREMENTS
To fit sizes 81-86 (91-97) (102-107) cm/32-34 (36-38) (40-42) in.
Actual measurements 90 (101) (112) cm/35½ (39¾) (44) in.
Side seam All sizes 46cm/18in.
Length to back neck 68 (70) (72) cm/26¾ (27½) (28¼) in.
Sleeve seam All sizes 30cm/11¾in.

MATERIALS
Pair of 4mm (No. 8) knitting needles. Yeoman yarn pack which contains 8 (9) (9) 100g balls of Yeoman Panama DK. Yeoman yarn packs cost £22.50 (£25) (£25), including p&p. We used Jeans (31), but other colours are available. For more yarn details, write to Yeoman Yarns Ltd, 36 Churchill Way, Fleckney, Leicestershire LE8 8UD, call 0116 240 4464, e-mail sales@yeomanyarns.co.uk or visit www.yeoman-yarns.co.uk

TENSION
22 stitches and 30 rows, to 10 x 10cm, over pattern lightly pressed, using 4mm needles.

ABBREVIATIONS
K, knit; p, purl; st, stitch; tog, together; p2togb, p2tog through back of sts; dec, decrease (by working 2 sts tog); skpo, slip 1, k1, pass slip st over.

NOTE
Yarn amounts are based on average requirements and are therefore approximate. Instructions are given for small size. Where they vary, work figures in round brackets for larger sizes. Instructions in square brackets are worked as stated after 2nd bracket.

LEFT FRONT

With 4mm needles, cast on 79 (85) (91) sts.
1st row: P1, [k1, p1] to end.
2nd row: P.
These 2 rows form pattern.
Pattern another 8 rows.
Shape side: 1st (dec) row: P1, skpo, pattern to end.
2nd row: P. **3rd row:** P1, k1, pattern to end.
4th to 10th rows: Repeat 2nd and 3rd rows, 3 times more, then work 2nd row again.
Repeat last 10 rows, 6 times more, then work 1st row again — 71 (77) (83) sts.
Pattern another 57 rows.
Shape armhole: Cast off 4 sts at beginning of next row and following alternate row. P 1 row.
Dec row: P1, skpo, pattern to end. P 1 row.
Repeat last 2 rows, 4 (6) (8) times more, then work dec row again — 57 (61) (65) sts.
Pattern another 51 (53) (55) rows.
Leave these sts on a spare needle.

RIGHT FRONT

With 4mm needles, cast on 79 (85) (91) sts.
Pattern 10 rows as given for left front.
Shape side: 1st (dec) row: Pattern to last 3 sts, k2tog, p1.
2nd row: P.
3rd row: Pattern to last 2 sts, k1, p1.
4th to 10th rows: Repeat 2nd and 3rd rows, 3 times more, then work 2nd row again.
Repeat last 10 rows, 6 times more, then work 1st row again — 71 (77) (83) sts. Pattern another 58 rows.

Shape armhole: Cast off 4 sts at beginning of next row and following alternate row.
Dec row: Pattern to last 3 sts, k2tog, p1. P 1 row.
Repeat last 2 rows, 4 (6) (8) times more, then work dec row again — 57 (61) (65) sts.
Pattern another 51 (53) (55) rows.
Do not break off the yarn. Leave these sts on a spare needle.

BACK

With 4mm needles, cast on 115 (127) (139) sts.
Pattern 10 rows as given for left front.
Shape sides: 1st (dec) row: P1, skpo, pattern to last 3 sts, k2tog, p1. **2nd row:** P.
3rd row: P1, k1, pattern to last 2 sts, k1, p1.
4th to 10th rows: Repeat 2nd and 3rd rows, 3 times more, then work 2nd row again.
Repeat last 10 rows, 6 times more, then work 1st row again — 99 (111) (123) sts.
Pattern another 57 rows.
Shape armholes: Cast off 4 sts at beginning of next 4 rows.
Dec row: P1, skpo, pattern to last 3 sts, k2tog, p1. P 1 row.
Repeat last 2 rows, 4 (6) (8) times more, then work dec row again — 71 (79) (87) sts.
Pattern another 51 (53) (55) rows.
Join shoulders: Place wrong side of right front to wrong side of back and with right side of back facing, cast off first 23 (25) (27) sts of back together with first 23 (25) (27) sts of right front by taking 1 st from each needle and working them tog, leave remaining 34 (36) (38) sts of right front on a st

referred to as up1, pattern to last st, up1, p1.

2nd row: P. **3rd row:** P1, k1, pattern to last 2 sts, k1, p1.

4th to 10th rows: Repeat 2nd and 3rd rows, 3 times more, then work 2nd row again.

Repeat last 10 rows, 6 times more, then work 1st row again — 81 (85) (89) sts.

Pattern another 9 rows.

Shape top: Cast off 4 sts at beginning of next 4 rows.

1st dec row: P1, skpo, pattern to last 3 sts, k2tog, p1. P 1 row.

Next row: P1, k1, pattern to last 2 sts, k1, p1. P 1 row.

Repeat last 4 rows, once more — 61 (65) (69) sts.

Work 1st dec row. P 1 row.

Repeat last 2 rows, 9 (10) (11) times more — 41 (43) (45) sts.

2nd dec row: P1, skpo, pattern to last 3 sts, k2tog, p1.

3rd dec row: P1, p2tog, p to last 3 sts, p2togb, p1.

Repeat last 2 rows, twice more — 29 (31) (33) sts. Cast off.

COLLAR

With right side facing, using 4mm needles and attached yarn, pattern 34 (36) (38) sts of right front, pick up and k1 st from right shoulder seam, pattern 25 (29) (33) sts of back neck, pick up and k1 st from left shoulder seam, pattern 34 (36) (38) sts of left front — 95 (103) (111) sts.

Pattern another 7 rows.

Increase row: Pattern 32 (36) (40), p into front, k into back, then p into front of next st — referred to as 3 from 1, [pattern 5, 3 from 1] 5 times, pattern 32 (36) (40) — 107 (115) (123) sts.

Pattern another 15 rows.

Cast off kwise.

BELT

With 4mm needles, cast on 9 sts. Work in pattern as given for left front until belt measures 135cm, ending with a 1st row. Cast off kwise.

TO MAKE UP

Set in sleeves. Join side and sleeve seams. Make belt loop in side seams.

> This jacket has set-in sleeves. It's knitted entirely in a broken rib stitch. The yarn is cotton and acrylic mix.

holder, slip next 25 (29) (33) sts of back on to spare needle. Place wrong side of left front to wrong side of back, slip first 34 (36) (38) sts of left front on to a st holder, rejoin yarn to back sts and cast off last 23 (25) (27) sts of back together with 23 (25) (27) sts of left front as before.

SLEEVES (BOTH ALIKE)

With 4mm needles, cast on 65 (69) (73) sts.

Pattern 10 rows as given for left front.

Shape sides: 1st (increase) row: P1, pick up loop lying between needles and k into back of it —

Your Good Health

Ask Dr Mel

Q I've been diagnosed with late-onset asthma — is it safe to exercise? I'm worried about getting breathless.

A People who have asthma often notice symptoms when they exercise. Asthma affects the tiny airways deep inside your lungs, making them inflamed and irritable and temporarily narrowed, producing breathlessness, wheezing and/or a cough. These symptoms can be triggered by viruses, allergies and drugs such as beta-blockers, as well as exercise, and many people with this condition avoid exercise because they're scared of an attack. But a recent review of research into aerobic exercise says that regular exercise and physical training, such as swimming and running, is actually good for people with asthma, as it improves cardiovascular fitness, lung function and general well-being.

So you can go ahead, provided your asthma is well-controlled and your GP agrees, but take a few precautions. If you're out of condition, start slowly, and gradually build up the intensity and duration; slow down if it seems too much. Always have your blue (reliever) inhaler to hand – you may find it helps to take a couple of puffs before you start. I'd also avoid strenuous exercise alone in remote places, in very cold weather, or when you have a virus infection.

TRY THIS Hula Hooping

There's now convincing evidence that people who exercise regularly are less depressed. Physical activity of almost any kind changes serotonin levels in the brain, helping you to feel more positive and less fatigued and irritable, and may also improve sleep. Hula hooping is ideal as you can do it indoors or outside. Make sure your hoop is weighted — it clings better to the body as you rotate — and the larger the diameter (eg, 40in if you're a dress size 10 to 14), the easier it is to master the technique.

HEALTH ON MY SHELF
Jennie Harding, aromatherapist

What's in your medicine cabinet?
Essential oils. Eucalyptus to freshen the air when I have a cold; lavender to help me sleep; tea tree for cuts — I put two drops on a tissue and apply straight away.

What's good in your fridge?
Organic cherry tomatoes. They're sweet and juicy. I eat them like fruit.

What's your favourite exercise?
Walking, especially where there are trees. I love them because they're tall and strong, and walking under them is peaceful.

What's a special treat?
Buying a nice notebook with good paper and a new pen to write my journal and jot down ideas for stories.

What makes you happy?
Being outside in sunshine and fresh air.

Any childhood remedy you still use?
A boiled egg with Marmite soldiers perks me up every time.

Jennie Harding is chief aromatherapist for Tisserand — visit www.tisserand.com.

TAKE 5...
Cope With Medical Tests

1 YOUR DOCTOR should explain the test, but read any information you're sent beforehand and don't hesitate to ask questions.

2 ASK IF YOU WILL BE provided with gowns and private changing facilities, as this can help preserve your dignity. Take a chaperone with you, if you wish.

3 TAKE SOMEONE with you (they may need to wait outside during the actual test).

4 TELL STAFF if you're in pain or feeling nervous/unwell during or after the test; they'll understand and help/reassure you.

5 MAKE SURE you know how and when you'll be given the results.

15 Monday

16 Tuesday

17 Wednesday

18 Thursday

19 Friday

20 Saturday

21 Sunday

Transfer Your Memories

Whether you went to Margate or Mauritius, turn your favourite holiday snaps into these fun mementoes of your trip

Cushion

VARIATIONS

✓ Add a ribbon or trim around the edge of the image for extra decoration, or pick out a detail by hand embroidering over it with coloured thread.

✓ Get creative and cut your image out instead of reproducing a square format — you could even cut out different parts of several photos to make up an eye-catching collage.

✓ Use multiples of square photos to make a mosaic-effect cushion cover — enlarge as big as you dare!

YOU WILL NEED

* White cotton or drill fabric
* White thread
* One A4 sheet of iron-on heat transfer paper for light fabrics, £5.80 for five, Crafty Computer Paper (0116 274 4755; www. craftycomputerpaper.co.uk)
* 23cm square feather cushion pad, £3.50, Design-A-Cushions (0131 539 0080; www.design-a-cushions.co.uk)
* A home computer with an inkjet colour printer
* Iron and ironing board
* Tape measure and pins
* Paper scissors
* Fabric scissors

Transfer a stand-out holiday photo into a small cushion, using iron-on transfer paper.

1 Select your image and crop it into a square on your computer. Resize it to 22cm, ensuring the image's resolution is 300dpi (dots per inch), so it appears sharp. Flip the image so that it's mirrored, using your computer programme or printer settings, then print on to a sheet of image transfer paper. Cut out, leaving a 5mm border all around the edge.

2 Cut out your fabric to 27 x 55cm and sew a single hem along one of the short edges. Lay your fabric on your ironing board, right side up, then place your printed image face down with the bottom of the image sitting 15cm up from the unhemmed short edge — ensure that it's equally spaced from the sides. Turn your iron to its hottest setting and run it over the paper for around 30-45 seconds, pressing down hard. Leave to cool for 5-10 minutes, and then carefully peel off.

3 Fold both ends of the fabric, sewn edge first, over the top of the image, until it measures 23cm from top to bottom, with the pattern sitting equally spaced from either end. Once this is in place, press the edges flat with your iron.

4 Mark a line of pins 2cm in from either of the raw edges and sew down both edges with your sewing machine. Clip the corners and turn the cushion right side out. Insert the cushion pad to complete.

Wall Art

Create some quirky wall art using water-slide transfers on wooden squares for a fun, retro look.

YOU WILL NEED

* Two sheets of white inkjet water-slide decal paper, £1.59 per sheet, Crafty Computer Paper (details, opposite)
* Three 12.7cm wooden birch plywood squares, £2.96 for three, Craft Shapes (07949 055733; www.craftshapes.co.uk)
* 2.5cm-wide satin ribbon in a coordinating colour to your photos
* A home computer with an inkjet colour printer
* White undercoat for wood and a paintbrush
* Scissors or a craft knife
* Sponge
* Old credit or store card to use as a scraper
* Gaffer tape
* Three panel pins and a hammer
* Needle and thread

1 Choose three photos that work well as a set and that would work in a square format. Crop them into 12.7cm squares, then

print on to transfer paper and cut out. If you're not confident on the computer, simply print them at a larger size in any format and cut them into squares of this size afterwards. Paint your wooden squares with white undercoat suitable for wood and leave to dry.

2 Place your first cut-out image into a tall glass of water and leave for about 30 seconds, until you're able to lift the image away from the backing paper. Don't allow it to over-soak or its stickiness will be reduced. While the image is soaking, take your first wooden square and dampen its front with water, using a sponge.

3 Peel back the image from the backing paper and place on the wooden square, adjusting into position by moving one corner at a time until the paper is in alignment with the wood. Once it's in place, take a credit card and gently rub it over the surface to smooth out any air bubbles. Repeat the process with your other two images. Leave to dry overnight.

Round off corners to follow the curves of the wood with scissors or a craft knife.

4 Take six 40cm-long pieces of ribbon and use gaffer tape to secure two lengths along the edges of the underside of each wooden square, then tie the ribbon into a bow. Wrap an extra strip of ribbon over the central knot and secure at the back with a few backstitches. Trim bow ends into a point. Hammer three nails in your wall, 16cm apart from each other, and hang images. If you don't want to mark your wall, you can use 3M Command Small Picture-hanging Strips (from B&Q, Homebase and www.solutions.3m.co.uk).

VARIATIONS

✓ Print a selection of images and layer them on a white ceramic jug.
✓ Transfer an image on to a candle — the image will burn down gradually.

Recipe For Disaster

Bella felt that, when it came to marriage, one needed to take a pragmatic view. But how could she get her sister to see sense?

You would not have thought to look at her that she was a witch. Bella had expected her to look at least "earthy", with trailing tresses and patchwork skirts. But this woman who introduced herself now was utterly ordinary. Even her name. When you would have expected a Morwenna or a Morganna, this witch was called Sue.

Bella couldn't keep the disappointment off her face.

The woman laughed. "Don't tell me," she said, "you were expecting someone with a pointy hat?"

Bella closed the property brochure she'd been poring over to make room for Sue and her laptop at the table.

"OK." Sue sat down. "Run me through it. It's your sister who's

Life without at least one pair of Jimmy Choos was not worth living

having difficulties?"

"Well... she is, but she just doesn't realise it," Bella said.

"Oh?"

"Faye — my sister — is going out with a complete loser. He doesn't work... well, not properly." Faye's new man was an artist. "And I've tried to make her see sense. Tried to make her see that what she needs is someone with earning potential." Bella felt that, when it came to marriage, one needed to take a pragmatic view. Life without at least one pair of Jimmy Choos was not a life worth living. She leaned towards Sue conspiratorially. "What she needs is someone like my Dan. He's as dull as ditchwater, of course. But steadily rising through the ranks, you know?"

Sue nodded again. "What you need then," she added, flipping the laptop open and tapping away, "is a spell."

Bella was handed a recipe for vegetable stew.

She read through the ingredients. Nothing terribly odd except, perhaps, tansy. Bella looked up. "Really?" she said. "Is this all that's required?"

Sue nodded. "Of course, you need to do a couple of things. You will need to get Faye and er..."

"Gary," Bella said.

"You'll need to get them both to eat the food."

"I could invite them for dinner."

"Exactly. But also," Sue continued, "while you're preparing the dish, you need to recite an incantation."

Bella made a face. "What, like 'abracadabra'?"

Sue laughed. "No. You just need to say what you want to happen. For example, you might say, 'Let the mismatched couple break up. Let the mismatched couple break up.'"

Bella nodded. "I see. And that's it?"

"That's it," Sue said, snapping her laptop shut.

As Bella stirred her stew later that month, she wondered whether she should have used something that resembled a cauldron. A saucepan didn't seem quite the ticket. But, as she stirred, she recited her incantation and closed her eyes, trying to believe she could make it happen.

Faye and Gary arrived as arranged, they ate their stew as arranged, and drank a cheap bottle of red with it.

Dan had tried to open a bottle of champagne but Bella had snatched it from his hands. "It's not for them," she hissed. She had bought it for a special occasion — the occasion when Dan finally got his promotion and they could

move into one of the five-bedroomed executive homes on the outskirts of the city that Bella had earmarked.

"But it's the first time we've had them both round," Dan said, looking at the bottle wistfully. "I thought—"

Bella ignored him and uncorked the red. She had ceased being interested in what Dan thought around the time he said, "I do".

Despite following the recipe to the letter, nothing happened. Not even the hint of an argument.

Finally, exasperated, Bella called Sue. "It's not worked," she said flatly.

Sue was silent for a moment on the other end. "Not worked, you say?"

"Not worked. Nothing. They're both still as entwined as two strands of bindweed."

Sue said, "That's funny. It usually works within a couple of weeks. Give me a call if nothing's happened by next Saturday."

"Oh, I will," Bella said. "I shall be ringing and asking for my money back."

It was then, as she put the phone back in its holder, she noticed the envelope, leaning up against the kettle. It was addressed to her in Dan's hand.

Dear Bella, it said. *After much thought, I have decided that I need my own space and have moved out. There is nobody else.*

Bella gasped. This was so out of character for Dan. She wondered what could have happened to have changed him. To make him so decisive. Then she read the next line, *For a while now, I have felt that we are mismatched...*

Mismatched? Mismatched! As if in a dream, she saw the fabulous five-bedroomed house with its *en suites* and landscaped gardens slip irretrievably from her perfectly manicured hands. "Nooo..." she wailed.

THE END
© Rachel Lovell

22 Monday

23 Tuesday

24 Wednesday

25 Thursday

26 Friday

27 Saturday

28 Sunday

PIECEWORD

Using the across clues to help you, transfer the jigsaw pieces into the blank grid to form a crossword that is symmetrical from top to bottom and left to right.

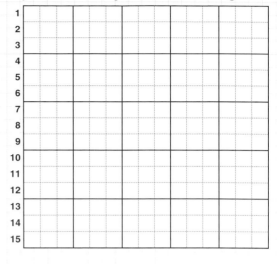

ACROSS
1 Couch • Wise old saying
3 Joint of the foot and leg • African deer-like animals
5 (Of fabric) like a City gent's suit (hyphenated) • Having no hair

7 Different • Paying (debts)
9 Small piece of matter • Long hilltop
11 Ireland's currency unit • End, finish
13 Paints in words • Male duck
15 Be without hope • Appeal to God

PATHFINDER

Beginning with the highlighted letter C, you must follow a continuous path through the letters to find 25 English counties. The trail passes through each and every letter once, and may twist up, down or sideways, but never diagonally.

AVON	LONDON
BUCKINGHAMSHIRE	MERSEYSIDE
CAMBRIDGESHIRE	NORFOLK
CHESHIRE	NORTHUMBERLAND
CLEVELAND	OXFORDSHIRE
CORNWALL	SHROPSHIRE
COUNTY DURHAM	SOMERSET
CUMBRIA	SOUTH YORKSHIRE
DEVON	SUFFOLK
DORSET	SURREY
HAMPSHIRE	WEST MIDLANDS
KENT	WILTSHIRE
LANCASHIRE	

Solutions to this month's puzzle on next month's puzzle

```
O S E R I E H S T M I D R E Y
U N O R H S C E W E A L R U M
T E R F O L K H I R N D S S E
H H I D T D U S T L I Y E S R
Y S P E E Y R H A M W S I O L
O A M V S T N U D E R I D F K
R H N O R E M O O D S H E F K
K S S H E S O C R R N O S U E
I H M I R I H E S O O D N O N
R E A R G E S T S F X U M L T
U B H E D I S P H R T H B L A
C N G A B R H O R O N L E R N
K I O V M A I R E C O L A C D
L C N A N C I H C N R N W U M
E V E L D E R S A A L A I R B
```

SOLUTIONS AUGUST, 2014

BLANKET, CUTTING, FREIGHT, KEEPING, KITCHEN
ATTIC

BEACH

29 Monday

30 Tuesday

1 Wednesday

2 Thursday

3 Friday

4 Saturday

5 Sunday

OCTOBER

6 Monday

7 Tuesday

8 Wednesday

9 Thursday

10 Friday

11 Saturday

12 Sunday

Give This Dog A Home!

Use your sewing machine to make this fun cushion in simple appliqué

YOU WILL NEED

* Access to a photocopier to enlarge template
* Tracing paper, pencil and fine black felt-tip pen
* Vilene Bondaweb
* 50cm of 137cm-wide pale turquoise wool fabric
* 20cm of 137cm-wide green/turquoise plaid wool fabric
* 25cm square of rust wool fabric
* 15 x 10cm piece of deep orange wool fabric
* 10cm square of black wool fabric
* 15cm square of lilac plaid wool fabric
* 20 x 15cm rectangle of light brown plaid herringbone wool fabric
* Air-erasable fabric pen
* Black stranded cotton embroidery thread
* Matching sewing threads
* 40cm square cushion pad

Note: Wool fabrics, from Mandors (0131 558 3888; www.mandors.co.uk).

Making the template

Enlarge the template on a photocopier by 300%. Then trace it onto tracing paper with a fine black felt-tip pen. Draw the smile on the muzzle.

CUTTING OUT

1 Turn the tracing paper to the wrong side. Trace the individual pieces onto the paper backing of the Bondaweb. Carefully cut out the paper pieces, leaving a margin of about 6mm around each piece.

2 Cut one 43 x 31cm rectangle for the front cushion and one 43cm square for the back cushion from pale turquoise wool fabric. Cut one 43 x 15cm rectangle for the band from green/turquoise plaid wool fabric.

3 Following the manufacturer's instructions, iron the Bondaweb pieces to the wrong side of the following fabrics: inner ear on green/turquoise plaid wool; body and outer ears on rust wool; head on deep orange wool; eyes and nose on black wool; ruff on lilac plaid wool and muzzle on light brown plaid herringbone wool fabric. Cut out the pieces accurately along the traced outlines.

TIP

We chose wool fabrics to give a soft, textured feel to our cushion, but most closely woven fabrics would be suitable — you could even introduce fur fabric for his muzzle or ruff.

Labels on template: Inner ear, Inner ear, Outer ear, Outer ear, Head, Eye, Eye, Ruff, Nose, Muzzle, Body

Template for Dog Cushion
Enlarge by 300% on a photocopier

TIP

To turn a corner when zigzag stitching, first stitch to the corner, then take your foot off the power and keep needle inserted at outer edge of corner. Lift presser foot and pivot fabric. Lower presser foot and continue stitching the next edge.

Making the front panel

1 With right sides facing and raw edges matching, pin and stitch one long edge of the band to one long edge of the front cushion, taking 1.5cm seam allowance. Press the seam open. Lay the front right side up on the ironing board with the band at the right-hand edge.

2 Peel Bondaweb paper backing off fabric pieces. Arrange body on cushion front, matching the straight edge to the lower edge, 10cm in from the left-hand edge. Press body in place to secure.

3 To position the other pieces, lay the template tracing on top of the body and slip the pieces underneath, matching their position on the tracing. Then remove and replace the tracing each time as you press the pieces in place in the following order: inner ears, head, outer ears, eyes, ruff, muzzle, nose.

4 Set the sewing machine to a close zigzag stitch, about 3mm wide. Using matching sewing threads, zigzag stitch pieces to the front cushion in the following order: inner ears, body, outer ears, head, eyes, ruff, muzzle and nose. Pull the threads to the wrong side and fasten with a knot.

5 Draw smile on the muzzle with an air-erasable fabric pen. Hand-stitch along drawn lines with backstitch, using four strands of black embroidery thread. With right sides facing and raw edges matching, join front and back cushion panels together round outer edge. Take 1.5cm seam allowance and leave a 20cm gap along one edge for turning through. Turn right side out, insert pad and slip stitch gap to close.

POST – CARD

Reader Rosemary Williams from Ely, Cambridgeshire, chooses Mount Maunganui in Tauranga, New Zealand

'Mount Maunganui is a beautiful spot in "the Land of the Long White Cloud" (the Maori name for New Zealand), with a deep harbour on one side and a surf beach on the other. It's situated on the east coast of the North Island and takes its name from the extinct volcanic cone that rises above the town. It's a true spot of paradise in a beautiful country!'

Mount Maunganui in Tauranga, New Zealand

POST – CARD

Reader Marian Williams, from Formby, Merseyside, nominates Dubrovnik in Croatia

Dubrovnik in Croatia

'My husband and I first visited Dubrovnik in 1973, and fell in love with the city's historic buildings, ancient walls, picturesque harbour and a sea so blue it hurt our eyes. We celebrated our 30th wedding anniversary there in 2005, and found the city, despite the bombing of 1991, renewed and vigorous. We returned this year for our son's wedding — a perfect day in a perfect setting!'

13 Monday

14 Tuesday

15 Wednesday

16 Thursday

17 Friday

18 Saturday

19 Sunday

Pumpkin & Orange Soup

SERVES *4*
CALORIES *320*
FAT *18g*
SATURATED FAT *3g*
SUITABLE FOR FREEZING *Yes*

INGREDIENTS

* 3 tablespoons good olive oil
* 1 onion, peeled and chopped
* 500g (1lb) pumpkin, peeled,
  deseeded and cubed
* 400g (14oz) sweet potatoes,
  peeled and chopped
* Finely grated zest and juice
  of 2 oranges
* 2 cloves garlic, peeled and sliced
* 1 teaspoon ground coriander
* 900ml (1½ pints) hot
  vegetable stock
* Salt and freshly ground
  black pepper
* 60g (2oz) pumpkin seeds
* Good pinch of sea salt
* Few sprigs of fresh coriander

1 Heat 2 tablespoons of the oil in a large pan. Add the onion and cook gently for 5 minutes, until softened.

2 Add the chopped pumpkin and sweet potatoes, the orange zest and juice, garlic and coriander, then pour in the vegetable stock. Season to taste. Bring to the boil, cover and simmer for 25 minutes until the pumpkin and sweet potato are tender.

3 Turn off the heat and use a stick blender to whizz the soup until it's really smooth.

4 Heat the remaining oil in a frying pan. Add the pumpkin seeds and sea salt. Cook for 2-3 minutes, shaking the pan, until the pumpkin seeds begin to pop and turn brown.

5 Serve the soup in warm bowls, sprinkled with the pumpkin seeds and a couple of coriander sprigs.

* Allow to cool, put into a rigid container, seal, label and freeze. Use within 2 months. Thaw in the fridge, and then reheat in a pan until piping hot.

TIP FROM OUR KITCHEN

Buy pumpkin seeds separately, as the ones you find in the centre of the pumpkin tend not be so tasty.

Your Good Health

Ask Dr Mel

Q My knee is often swollen and painful. Would a steroid injection help, and for how long would it relieve the pain?

A A hot red joint requires immediate assessment as it could be due to infection that can cause rapid and permanent damage (or you could have gout or inflammation such as rheumatoid arthritis). But less dramatic pain and swelling can be due to osteoarthritis, cartilage/ligament damage, or bursitis caused by irritation or overuse — for example, "housemaid's knee". So you need an examination, and possibly an X-ray or MR scan to see what's wrong, and whether surgery would help. Try ice-packs (towel-wrapped, for 15 minutes, four times a day), rest, painkillers or non-steroidal anti-inflammatory drugs such as ibuprofen, and a support bandage to make it feel better. Physiotherapy may help to settle things down.

But if these don't work, and your GP thinks there's some inflammation, a steroid injection (including some local anaesthetic) may help. Injections are often effective and can relieve pain for months or even permanently; a second one can usually be given if necessary. But it's not clear whether frequent injections can weaken the joint, so if symptoms persist, you may need referring to a specialist.

TRY THIS — RICE For Pain Relief

No, not a dish served with curry, but an acronym used by physios for the safest, most effective way to deal with shoulder pain in the early stages. Rest the shoulder for 48 hours; put an Ice pack on the painful area four to eight times a day for 20 minutes. (Never place the ice directly on the skin; wrap it in a towel.) If there is swelling, wrap the shoulder up to Compress it and keep your shoulder Elevated, using a pillow as support.

HEALTH ON MY SHELF
Becki Houlston, life coach

What's in your medicine cabinet?
Vitamin D3, as I have to be careful in the sun, antioxidants and rosehip oil.

What's good in your fridge?
Barley grass — it tastes revolting, but I add it to fruit juices to keep my innards happy.

What's your favourite exercise?
I love rowing, either in a kayak in the sea, or in the gym. Yoga is also an important part of my health routine.

What's a special treat?
Black cod (available from Japanese supermarkets) marinated in miso and pickled stem ginger. It's really delicious.

If you can't sleep, what works?
Lavender oil and deep breathing. And if I have something on my mind, I write it down.

Any major health wake-up calls?
Five skin cancers in the past two years have taught me that my health — mental, physical, spiritual — is hugely important.

Any childhood remedy you still use?
A hug.

TAKE 5...
Lumps To Show Your GP

1 ANY BREAST LUMP, regardless of how it feels, but be aware that most lumps are not breast cancer — it's more likely to be benign.

2 ANY LUMP ON OR UNDER THE SKIN should be shown to a medical professional.

3 ANY LUMP IN THE NECK, armpit or groin, lasting more than 2 weeks (glands often swell in these areas when we have a sore throat or skin infection).

4 ANY LUMP THAT IS FOUND in the tummy or genitals.

5 ANY MOUTH LUMP or ulcer that is very painful or lasts for more than 3 weeks — also see a doctor if you are getting mouth ulcers regularly.

20 Monday

21 Tuesday

22 Wednesday

23 Thursday

24 Friday

25 Saturday

26 Sunday

Kids' Club

Cool kids can earn their stripes with these brightly coloured knits

---

MEASUREMENTS

To fit ages 5-6 (7-8) (9-10) years.
Actual measurements 73 (80) (86)
cm/28¾ (31½) (34) in.
Sleeve seam 30 (32.5) (35) cm/11¾
(12¾) (13¾) in.
Girl's sweater: Side seam 21.5 (23)
(24) cm/8½ (9) (9½) in.
Length 38 (40.5) (43) cm/15 (16) (17) in.
Boy's sweater: Side seam 26.5 (28)
(29) cm/10½ (11) (11½) in.
Length 43 (45) (48) cm/17 (17¾) (19) in.

MATERIALS

Girl's sweater: 2 (2) (2) 100 g balls of
King Cole Magnum Chunky in Violet
(314), 1 (2) (2) ball(s) in Rouge (009)
and 1 ball in Charcoal (187).

Boy's sweater: 2 (3) (3) 100 g balls
of King Cole Magnum Chunky in
Bluebell (299) and 2 (2) (3) balls in
Charcoal (187).
Both items: No. 1 (7½mm) and No. 0
(8mm) knitting needles. For stockists,
write to: King Cole Ltd, Merrie Mills,
Elliott Street, Silsden, Keighley, West
Yorkshire BD20 0DE. Call 01535
650230, fax 01535 650240 or visit
www.kingcole.co.uk.

TENSION

12 stitches and 16 rows, to 10 x 10cm,
over stocking stitch, using No. 0
(8mm) needles.

ABBREVIATIONS

K, knit; **p,** purl; **st,** stitch; **tog,**
together; **dec,** decrease (by taking 2
sts tog); **ss,** stocking st (k on right side
and p on wrong side); **skpo, slip1,** k1,
pass slip st over.

NOTE

Yarn amounts are based on
average requirements and are
therefore approximate. Instructions
are given for small size. Where they
vary, work figures in round brackets
for larger sizes. Instructions in square
brackets are worked as stated after
2nd bracket.

Girl's Sweater

BACK

With No. 1 (7½mm) needles and
Violet, cast on 45 (49) (53) sts.
1st rib row: K1, [p1, k1] to end.
2nd rib row: P1, [k1, p1] to end.
Repeat last 2 rows, once more.
Change to No. 0 (8mm) needles.
Beginning with a k row, work in
ss and stripe pattern of
2 rows Rouge, 4 rows Violet,
2 rows Charcoal, 4 rows Rouge,
2 rows Violet, 4 rows Rouge,
2 rows Charcoal, 4 rows Violet
throughout until 30 (32) (34) rows
of striped pattern have been
worked.
Mark each end of last row for side
seams. **
Pattern another 26 (28) (30) rows.
Shape shoulders: Next row:
With Charcoal (Rouge) (Rouge),
cast off 12 (13) (14) sts, slip centre
21 (23) (25) sts on to st holder

(including st used in casting off),
rejoin Charcoal (Rouge) (Rouge)
and cast off last 12 (13) (14) sts.

FRONT

Work as back to **. Pattern
another 18 (20) (22) rows.
Shape neck: Next row: K18 (19)
(20), turn and work on these sts
for left side neck.
Left side neck: Dec 1 st at neck
edge on next 6 rows — 12 (13)
(14) sts.
Pattern 1 row. Cast off.
Right side neck: With right side
facing, slip centre 9 (11) (13) sts
on to a st holder, rejoin
appropriate yarn to remaining sts
and k to end — 18 (19) (20) sts.
Dec 1 st at neck edge on next 6
rows — 12 (13) (14) sts.
Pattern 1 row. Cast off.

SLEEVES (BOTH ALIKE)

With No. 1 (7½mm) needles and
Violet, cast on 23 (25) (27) sts.

1st rib row: K1, [p1, k1] to end.
2nd rib row: P1, [k1, p1] to end.
Change to No. 0 (8mm) needles.
Beginning with a k row, ss 2 rows.
Continue in ss and stripe pattern
of 2 rows Rouge, 4 rows Violet,
2 rows Charcoal, 4 rows Rouge,
2 rows Violet, 4 rows Rouge,
2 rows Charcoal, 4 rows Violet
throughout, increasing 1 st at
each end of first row and 6 (7)
(8) following 6th rows — 37 (41)
(45) sts.
Pattern another 7 (5) (3) rows.
Cast off.

NECKBAND

Join right shoulder seam.
With right side facing and using
Rouge (Violet) (Rouge) and No. 1
(7½mm) needles, pick up and k7
sts down left front neck, k9 (11)
(13) sts from centre front neck,
pick up and k7 sts up right front
neck, 1 st down right back neck,
k21 (23) (25) sts from centre back

neck, then pick up and k1 st up
left back neck — 46 (50) (54) sts.
Work 2 rows in k1, p1 rib.
Cast off in rib.

TO MAKE UP

Press as given on ball band. Join
left shoulder and neckband
seam. Sew on sleeves between
markers on back and front. Taking
half a st into the seam, join side
and sleeve seams.

Boy's Sweater

BACK

With No. 1 (7½mm) needles and
Bluebell, cast on 45 (49) (53) sts.
1st rib row: K1, [p1, k1] to end.
2nd rib row: P1, [k1, p1] to end.
Repeat last 2 rows, once more.
Change to No. 0 (8mm) needles.
Beginning with a k row, work in
ss and stripe pattern of 4 rows
Charcoal and 4 rows Bluebell
throughout until 38 (40) (42)
rows of striped pattern have
been worked.
Mark each end of last row for side
seams. **
Pattern another 26 (28) (30) rows.
Shape shoulders: Next row: With
Bluebell (Charcoal) (Bluebell), cast
off 12 (13) (14) sts, slip centre 21
(23) (25) sts (including st used in
casting off) on to st holder, rejoin
Bluebell (Charcoal) (Bluebell) and
cast off last 12 (13) (14) sts.

FRONT

Work as back to **. Pattern
another 18 (20) (22) rows.
Shape neck: Next row: K18 (19)
(20), turn and work on these sts
for left side neck.
Left side neck: Dec 1 st at neck
edge on next 6 rows — 12 (13)
(14) sts.
Pattern 1 row. Cast off.
Right side neck: With right side
facing, slip centre 9 (11) (13) sts
on to a st holder, rejoin
appropriate yarn to remaining

sts and k to end — 18 (19) (20) sts.
Dec 1 st at neck edge on next 6
rows — 12 (13) (14) sts.
Pattern 1 row. Cast off.

SLEEVES (BOTH ALIKE)

With No. 1 (7½mm) needles and
Bluebell, cast on 23 (25) (27) sts.
1st rib row: K1, [p1, k1] to end.
2nd rib row: P1, [k1, p1] to end.
Change to No. 0 (8mm) needles.
Beginning with a k row, ss 2 rows.
Continue in ss and stripe pattern
of 4 rows Charcoal and 4 rows
Bluebell throughout, increasing
1 st at each end of first row
and 6 (7) (8) following 6th rows —
37 (41) (45) sts.
Pattern another 7 (5) (3) rows.
Cast off.

NECKBAND

Join right shoulder seam.
With right side facing and using
Charcoal (Bluebell) (Charcoal) and
No. 1 (7½mm) needles, pick up
and k7 sts down left front neck, k9
(11) (13) sts from centre front neck,
pick up and k7 sts up right front
neck, 1 st down right back neck,
k21 (23) (25) sts from centre back
neck, then pick up and k1 st up
left back neck — 46 (50) (54) sts.
Work 2 rows in k1, p1 rib.
Cast off in rib.

TO MAKE UP

Press as given on ball band. Join
left shoulder seam and neckband.
Sew on sleeves between markers
on back and front. Taking half a
st into the seam, join side and
sleeve seams.

Safety First

I didn't realise our car went this slowly. I didn't think it was possible. And that's fine, as this is as fast as I'm prepared to go!

"John..?"

"What?" I snap, as I glance in the rear-view mirror. "I was just about to pull out."

My wife smiles weakly. "Drive carefully."

I open my mouth, then I remember what she's been through and I shut up. I inhale and look around to see if anyone is pulling out of the car park. Nothing. I check again. You can't be too careful. Still no movement, so I stick my foot on the clutch, put the car into first, come up on the accelerator and ease the car from the space. Out of the corner of my eye, I see movement and immediately slam my foot on the brake. I'm aware of my wife's eyes on me.

A woman is returning to her car. I reverse and wait for her to pull out. Then I wipe sweaty palms on my trousers and check again. We reach the barrier without incident. I pull through it, indicate, turn right and roll down the slope to the hospital gates. Here comes the tricky bit. Driving on main roads. Left or right? I hesitate. Left. That way I can avoid the bypass, the road where the speed limit is a number to ignore.

"OK, John?"

I jump at Louise's voice. I'd almost forgotten she was there. "Fine."

My heartbeat races as we get on the main road. It is mid-morning, so the traffic should be fairly light. The next left on to a smaller road is also quiet. But I can't help my fingers tightening on the wheel as a car passes us. What if the driver is still drunk from the night before? What if the car isn't roadworthy? I give myself a shake. I never used to think like this.

I drop down a gear as I approach the give-way lines and stop. This is a bad corner. You need to pull out before you can see if anything is coming from the right. Why didn't I think of this earlier?

I didn't realise our car went so slowly. I didn't think it was mechanically possible, but it is. I've never driven so slowly, that's for sure. At approximately two miles per hour, the car creeps across the give-way line,

I jump at Louise's voice. I'd almost forgotten she was there

while I crane my head to the right. It's clear, so I pull out.

The road carries us fairly smoothly, with the occasional bump that I can't avoid, to the roundabout. Louise winces with every bump. A car is approaching on the opposite road and, whereas I'd normally carry on, I stop and wait a few seconds for him to pass, then I manoeuvre around the roundabout.

My eyes scan the road ahead. As the road bends to the left, I notice a lorry parked on our side of the road. A huge lorry with its hazard lights flashing. One by one the cars in front drive around it. On the wrong side of the road. There are suddenly no cars left and it's our turn to pass. .

I inhale. How many times have I done this before? Stacks. Usually without thinking. But then I didn't have such a precious cargo on board.

As I did on the give-way lines, I creep out and brake sharply. There's a car coming towards us. A quick look at the space between the front of our car and the opposite pavement tells me he has enough space to pass safely. But I still hold my breath. While the road is clear, I pull out and we're on our way again.

Traffic lights provide my next concern. Green as we approach. It will change any second. I know it will. As I pass it goes to amber and I panic. What if the car behind jumps the lights and runs into us? I wait for the bump. It doesn't happen.

We're about two minutes from home. I force myself not to relax. Most accidents happen near home, on roads that we're most familiar with. I indicate right and slow down. Louise had a bump here two years ago. She stopped as a car was pulling out of this narrow junction and the car behind her didn't stop. I glance in the mirror, see Louise and a car approaching us. It slows. Both roads are clear and I pull into the junction and onto the road that leads home. Never have I been so grateful to get here.

As I stop outside our home, I feel sweat trickle across my brow. My hands are shaking. I have no time to congratulate myself on a job well done as Louise's door opens. I leap out and hold out one hand to help her out. She winces. Together we walk to the other back door. We open it and stare at the back seat. There's a squawk from inside.

Louise makes an "It's-all-over-to-you" gesture, then she steps back and leaves me staring at the tiny car seat we struggled to fit at the hospital. As I lean in, I get a waft of new-baby smell and I feel my nerves start to prickle again. Driving home was a doddle. What was I worried about? The hard part is about to start. How on earth are we going to cope with our one-day-old daughter?

THE END
© Joanne Lloyd

27 Monday

28 Tuesday

29 Wednesday

30 Thursday

31 Friday

1 Saturday

2 Sunday

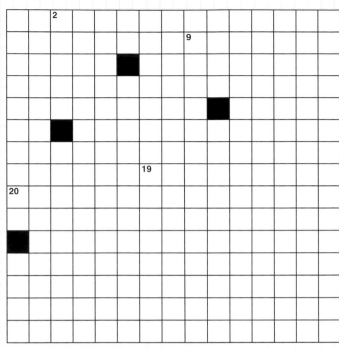

SKELETON

Have double the fun with this puzzle — you've got to fill in the answers and the black squares! We've given you the bare bones to start and it will help you to know that the black squares in the finished grid form a symmetrical pattern.

ACROSS
1 Diabolical, infernal
5 Picture cut up into pieces to be fitted together
10 Person who prefers not to associate with others
11 Articles made of tin, copper etc
12 Gradual appearance
13 Opposite of 'under'
15 Impious, profane
17 Vehicle's front light
20 Regarding with approval
21 Number of months in a year
22 Children's board-game
24 Subsection
28 Evening entertainment venue
29 Aspect, viewpoint
30 Roving
31 Pointed tools for knitting

DOWN
1 God be praised!
2 Jousting weapon
3 Abnormal
4 Person as opposed to an animal
6 Snow house
7 Hold up progress by delaying tactics
8 Ship's stern trail
9 Become harder to climb
14 Struck dumb
16 Fast food in a bun
18 Lower the rank of
19 Unskilfully
23 Frequently
25 Small red-breasted bird
26 Cherub
27 A single time

VOWEL PLAY

Fill in the missing vowels to the clues given to complete this crossword with a difference.

ACROSS
1 NSTHTC (11)
8 MSR (5)
9 NGLGS (9)
11 NRSMDS (10)
12 ZNC (4)
14 CMPS (5)
16 LLGTTN (3-6)
18 LNDNR (4,2,3)
20 LSPS (5)
22 GLY (4)
23 PCNCKNG (10)
27 LPMNT (9)
28 CDT (5)
29 SYNTHSSR (11)

DOWN
2 NSTRM (7)
3 R (5)
4 TNTTV (9)
5 GGD (5)
6 X (4)
7 DMST (6)
8 MNCLTR (11)
10 SCNDSGHT (6,5)
13 FWL (4)
15 SCN (4)
17 LRGNTT (9)
19 NLSN (6)
21 SPNDL (7)
24 NRT (5)
25 CCT (5)
26 DNY (4)

Solutions to this month's puzzle on next month's puzzle

SOLUTIONS FOR SEPTEMBER, 2014

NOVEMBER

Man's Sweater And Scarf

Keep the man in your life warm and stylish with this cosy set

MEASUREMENTS
Sweater: *To fit sizes 91-97 (102-107) (112-117) cm/36-38 (40-42) (44-46) in.*
Actual measurements *104 (117) (129) cm/41 (46) (50¾) in.*
Side seam *44 (45.5) (47) cm/ 17¼ (18) (18½) in.*
Length to shoulder *67 (70) (73) cm/26¼ (27½) (28¾) in.*
Sleeve seam *47 (49) (53) cm/18½ (19¼) (21) in.*
Scarf: *27 x 117cm/10½ x 46in.*

MATERIALS
Sweater: *12 (13) (14) 50g balls of Sirdar Country Style DK. 3¾mm (No. 9) and 4mm (No. 8) knitting needles; a 3¾mm (No. 9) circular needle; cable needle.*

Scarf: *4 x 50g balls of Sirdar Country Style DK. 4mm (No. 8) knitting needles; cable needle.*
Both items: *We used Chocolate (530). For yarn stockists, write to: Sirdar Spinning Ltd, Flanshaw Lane, Alverthorpe, Wakefield, West Yorkshire WF2 9ND. Call 01924 371501.*

TENSION
25 stitches and 28 rows, to 10 x 10cm, over rib when slightly stretched, using 4mm needles.

ABBREVIATIONS
K, *knit;* **p,** *purl;* **st,** *stitch;* **tog,** *together;* **inc,** *increase (by working twice into same st);* **dec,** *decrease (by taking 2sts tog);* **skpo,***slip 1, k1, pass slip st over;* **c4b,** *slip next 2 sts on to cable needle and leave at back,* **k2,** *then k2 from cable needle;* **c4f,** *slip next 2 sts on to cable needle and leave at front, k2, then k2 from cable needle.*

NOTE
Yarn amounts are based on average requirements and are therefore approximate. Instructions are given for small size. Where they vary, work figures in round brackets for larger sizes. Instructions in square brackets are worked as stated after 2nd bracket.

BACK

With 4mm needles, cast on 130 (146) (162) sts.
1st row: P3, [k4, p4] to last 7 sts, k4, p3.
2nd row: K3, [p4, k4] to last 7 sts, p4, k3.
3rd and 4th rows: As 1st and 2nd rows.
5th row: P3, [k4, p4] 4 (4) (5) times, c4b, p4, [k4, p4] 6 (8) (8) times, c4f, [p4, k4] 4 (4) (5) times, p3.
6th row: As 2nd row.
These 6 rows form pattern.
Pattern another 118 (122) (126) rows.
Shape armholes: Cast off 2 sts at beginning of next 2 rows.
Dec row: P1, k3, skpo, pattern to last 6 sts, k2tog, k3, p1.
Next row: K1, p4, pattern to last 5 sts, p4, k1.
Repeat last 2 rows, 6 times more, then work dec row again — 110 (126) (142) sts.
Pattern another 47 (51) (55) rows.
Shape shoulders: Next row: Cast off 29 (35) (41) sts, pattern to last 29 (35) (41) sts, cast off last 29 (35) (41) sts. Leave remaining 52 (56) (60) sts on a st holder.

FRONT

With 4mm needles, cast on 130 (146) (162) sts.
1st row: P3, [k4, p4] to last 7 sts, k4, p3.
2nd row: K3, [p4, k4] to last 7 sts, p4, k3.
3rd and 4th rows: As 1st and 2nd rows.
5th row: P3, [k4, p4] 4 (4) (5) times,c4b, p4, [k4, p4] 6 (8) (8) times, c4f, [p4, k4] 4 (4) (5) times, p3.
6th row: As 2nd row.
These 6 rows form pattern.
Pattern another 100 (104) (108) rows.
Shape neck: Next row: Pattern 65 (73) (81), turn and work on these sts only for left side neck.
Left side neck: Pattern 1 row.
Dec 1 st at neck edge on next row and 7 following alternate rows — 57 (65) (73) sts. Pattern 1 row.
Shape armhole: Next row: Cast off 2, pattern to last 2 sts, work 2tog.
Pattern 1 row.
Dec row: P1, k3, skpo, pattern to last 2 sts, work 2tog.
Next row: Pattern to last 5 sts, p4, k1.
Repeat last 2 rows, 6 times more, then work dec row again — 38 (46) (54) sts.

Shape top: Cast off 2 sts at beginning of next 2 rows.
Dec row: P1, k3, skpo, pattern to last 6 sts, k2tog, k3, p1.
Next row: K1, p4, pattern to last 5 sts, p4, k1.
Repeat last 2 rows, 6 times more, then work dec row again — 78 (86) (94) sts. Pattern 1 row. Cast off 5 sts at beginning of next 2 rows and 4 sts at beginning of next 12 (14) (16) rows — 20 sts.
Cast off.

COLLAR

Join shoulder seams. With right side facing and using 3¾mm circular needle, pick up and k57 (59) (61) sts up right front neck, rib 52 (56) (60) sts at back neck, then pick up and k57 (59) (61) sts down left front neck — 166 (174) (182) sts.
Work backwards and forwards in rows.
Next row: P1 (5) (1), [k4, p4] to last 5 (9) (5) sts, k4, p1 (5) (1).
Next row: K1 (5) (1), p4, [k4, p4] to last 1 (5) (1) st(s), k1 (5) (1).
Repeat last 2 rows, 8 (9) (10) times more. Cast off in pattern.

TO MAKE UP

Set in sleeves, then join side and sleeve seams. Overlapping left over right, sew row-end edges of collar to neck at centre front.

Pattern 1 row.
Dec 1 st at neck edge only on next row and 8 (10) (12) following 4th rows — 29 (35) (41) sts.
Pattern another 13 (9) (5) rows.
Cast off.
Right side neck: With right side facing, rejoin yarn to remaining sts and pattern to end — 65 (73) (81) sts. Pattern 1 row.
Dec 1 st at neck edge on next row and 8 following alternate rows — 56 (64) (72) sts.
Shape armhole: Cast off 2 sts at beginning of next row.
Dec row: Work 2tog, pattern to last 6 sts, k2tog, k3, p1.
Next row: K1, p4, pattern to end.
Repeat last 2 rows, 6 times more, then work dec row again — 38 (46) (54) sts. Pattern 1 row.

Dec 1 st at neck edge only on next row and 8 (10) (12) following 4th rows — 29 (35) (41) sts.
Pattern another 13 (9) (5) rows.
Cast off.

SLEEVES (BOTH ALIKE)

With 4mm needles, cast on 66 (74) (82) sts.
1st row: P3, [k4, p4] to last 7 sts, k4, p3.
2nd row: K3, [p4, k4] to last 7 sts, p4, k3.
These 2 rows form pattern.
Pattern another 2 (6) (8) rows.
Working extra sts into pattern as they occur, inc 1 st at each end of next row and 15 following 8th rows — 98 (106) (114) sts.
Pattern another 7 (11) (19) rows.

TO MAKE

With 4mm needles, cast on 68 sts.
1st row (wrong side): P4, [k4, p4] to end.
2nd row: K4, [p4, k4] to end.
3rd row: As 1st row.
4th row: [K4, p4] 4 times, c4b, [p4, k4] 4 times.
5th and 6th rows: As 1st and 2nd rows.
These 6 rows form pattern.
Repeat these 6 rows, 54 times more, then work 1st row again.
Cast off in pattern.

POST – CARD

Egypt

Reader Faith Burke, from Deal in Kent, nominates the enduring magic of Egypt

'I love Egypt, where the culture and traditions still exist among the people. You can see them fishing on the River Nile in little boats. The ancient monuments you can visit are truly spectacular — from the Pyramids of Giza, Abu Simbel (left) to The Valley of the Kings at Luxor — while the people are warm, friendly and very pleased to welcome tourists to their country.'

POST – CARD

Rochester in Kent

Reader Caroline Ellis, from Belvedere in Kent, recommends Rochester, also in Kent

'There's nothing I enjoy more than "antiquing" in the shops on Rochester's historic High Street. There's also a glorious cathedral and a Norman castle with views along the River Medway. The town's all the better for still being a working place, rather than simply a tourist trap…though there are many echoes of Dickens, of course. I end my day's browsing with home-made cake in an upstairs tea shop.'

3 Monday

4 Tuesday

5 Wednesday

6 Thursday

7 Friday

8 Saturday

9 Sunday

Have a go at..
Needle Felting

Create a gorgeous needle case using this surprisingly easy method

Needle felting requires little skill and few materials, and the results are instant. The simple technique involves barbed needles stabbing in and out of wool causing the fibres to bond, mat and turn to felt. The resulting felt can be used to create pictures, objects and three-dimensional items.

All you need are felting needles, a dense foam sponge to work on and coloured wool tops (carded wool fleece that's ready for spinning). Merino wool is the best quality for needle felting. When using the wool, never cut it, just pull off tufts and wisps.

Felting needles are long, thin and very sharp. Their tiny barbs catch the wool and interlock the fibres to felt them together. They're prone to bend, and will break eventually, so always have a few to hand.

They're also available in different sizes — 38 gauge is a versatile size and is what we used to make this needle case.

You can use the needles without a holder but they're more comfortable to use when fixed in a handle and less prone to going astray. Single-needle handles are available but a multi-needle handle gives the option of using more than one needle at once.

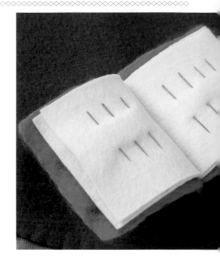

YOU WILL NEED

* Felting needles*
* Multi-needle holder*
* Dense foam sponge (approximately 5cm thick, 21 x 15cm*)
* 20g of turquoise wool top*
* 5g of sepia, candy pink, cerise, green and bright yellow wool tops*
* Dressmaking pins
* Assorted sequins
* Sewing thread to match sequins
* 20cm square of ready-made yellow felt
* Yellow stranded cotton embroidery thread
* Large crewel embroidery needle
* Air-erasable pen

*Note: A needle-felting kit consisting of sponge, four needles and multi-needle holder costs £7.15; wool tops, 100g for £3.95, both from www. gilliangladrag.co.uk (01306 898144)

To make

1 Use the air-erasable pen to mark out an 18 x 9cm rectangle centrally on the foam sponge. Then pull off tufts of turquoise wool and lay them across the foam, folding or tucking the wispy ends within the drawn rectangle. Do not cut ends. Continue to build up a thin layer of wool.

2 With four needles fixed in a multi-needle holder, stab the wool fibres repeatedly. The fibres will compact as you work.

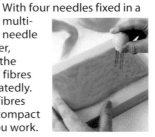

Add more wool at right angles to the first and stab again. Carefully lift the rectangle, turn it over and repeat. Gradually add more wool, in the same way, to increase the thickness and define its shape, turning it over from time to time until you have a dense, even rectangle for the needle-case cover. As a guide, it should be approximately 5mm thick and lift cleanly off the foam.

3 Insert a few dressmaking pins into the rectangle to form a line 8cm from the right-hand short edge. This will define the front of the cover. Referring to the main picture, opposite, use the air-erasable pen to draw the bird and branch shape. Pull off a wisp of sepia wool and lay the wool across the front cover to form a branch. Use a single felting

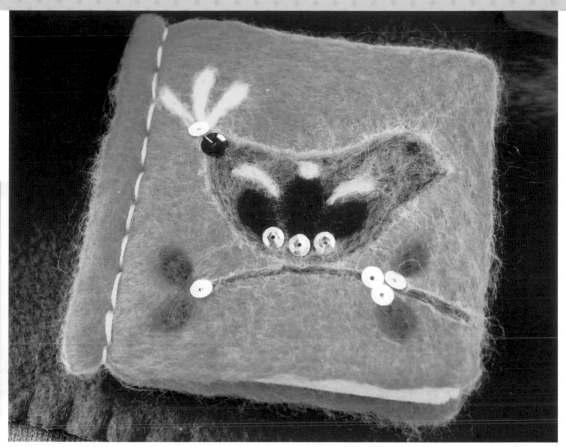

needle to stab the branch to the cover. Fold the extending end of the wool back along the branch and stab in place. Continue stabbing the wool to secure the branch.

4 Arrange tufts of candy pink wool within the bird shape. Stab the outline of the bird with a single felting needle, then fill in the shape, adding more wool a little at a time to build up the shape.

5 Pull off wisps of cerise wool. Roll one wisp into a ball for the eye and needle it in position on the bird. Bend another wisp into a loop and place on the centre of the bird. Stab the loop, then the

ends, to make a teardrop shape. Fill in the shape with more wool, then repeat on each side of the centre teardrop. Add wisps of green wool to make leaves on the branch, outlining the shapes, then filling them in with wool.

6 Pull off wisps of yellow wool. Roll one wisp in a ball and needle to the bird above the centre teardrop. Arrange a yellow wisp in a curve above each side teardrop and stab in place. Apply three tail feathers with wisps of yellow wool, stabbing them in place and adding a little more wool to thicken the tips.

7 Highlight the bird and branch with a few sequins, sewing them to the front with a single length of sewing thread. Cut four 8cm squares of yellow ready-made felt for the

pages. Fold the cover in half, slip the pages inside, butting the edges against the fold. Tack the layers together.

Sew a "hinge" through the layers along the pinned line with backstitch, using four strands of stranded cotton embroidery thread.

TIPS
✓ Felting needles are extremely sharp, so always watch what you're doing.
✓ Work on a protected, flat, stable surface, not your lap.
✓ Always insert your needle straight down into your work.
✓ Use a stencil (eg, a cookie cutter) to create shapes such as flowers or birds. Place the wool in the cutter, then needle it to fill the shape.

Your Good Health

Ask Dr Mel

Q I lost my sense of smell a few weeks ago – what can I do to make it come back?

A The most likely cause is a recent cold; colds and allergies such as hay fever produce congestion in the delicate membranes that line our nasal passages. They also trigger sneezing, and congestion in the sinuses behind the nose, which become filled with catarrh instead of air. Even though colds clear up in a week or so, your sinuses can remain congested for some time, and you may have noticed facial pain, headaches, "blocked" ears, or a reduced sense of taste, too.

Try a decongestant nasal spray for up to a week, or decongestant tablets from your pharmacist (provided your blood pressure is normal). Steam inhalations (take care not to scald yourself!) may also help. If you think you could have an allergy, antihistamine tablets and/or a steroid nasal spray from your pharmacy are also worth a try.

But if your sense of smell doesn't return in a couple of weeks, see your GP. You could have a blockage in the front or back of your nose, such as polyps (benign fleshy growths, often linked to allergies), or (much less likely) something wrong with the nerves or brain areas that detect smell, in which case you would have to see a specialist.

TRY THIS Meditation

As often as you can, find somewhere quiet (indoors or outside) where you know you won't be disturbed. Sit in a comfortable chair, close your eyes and focus first on the sounds, sensations and smells around you, and then on your breathing, making it as slow and even as you can. If any thoughts come into your mind, try to ignore them. If you find this hard, then start off with just a one-minute meditation and increase it as you get better at switching off. And throughout the day, take a deeper, slower breath every 20 minutes.

HEALTH ON MY SHELF

Dr Nerina Ramlakhan, sleep and energy therapist

What's in your medicine cabinet?
Arnica and magnesium to help speed up muscle recovery after a training session. Bach Rescue Remedy, for moments when I might be feeling a bit wobbly.

What's good in your fridge?
Chia seeds. They're high in omega-3 fats, amino acids, antioxidants and potassium. I sprinkle them on my porridge.

What's your favourite exercise?
I love swimming, cycling and running.

What's a special treat?
Lemon drizzle cake.

If you can't sleep, what works?
Telling myself that I'm just going to rest. The key is not to stress about it.

Any childhood remedies you still use?
A dab of eucalyptus oil my pillow. I'm sure it's associated with comfort and thoughts of my mum, who used it, too.
Nerina is Silentnight's Sleep Expert (www. silentnight.co.uk).

TAKE 5...
Ways To Take Medicines Safely

1 READ THE LABEL and also the information leaflet.

2 TELL YOUR GP if you find it difficult to stick to the timings; it may be possible to adjust them.

3 REMIND YOURSELF to take your medicines by setting an alarm.

4 IF YOU TAKE SEVERAL MEDICINES, consider using a pill organiser box, marked with days and times.

5 CHECK WITH YOUR PHARMACIST if you miss one or more doses, take an extra tablet by mistake, or vomit soon after taking medication.

10 Monday

11 Tuesday

12 Wednesday

13 Thursday

14 Friday

15 Saturday

16 Sunday

Family Pasta Bake

SERVES 6
CALORIES 420
FAT 28g
SATURATED FAT 14g
SUITABLE FOR FREEZING No

INGREDIENTS

* 1 tablespoon olive oil
* 2 onions, peeled and chopped
* 2 cloves garlic, peeled and crushed
* 500g (1lb) minced beef
* 1 aubergine, chopped
* 2 tablespoons tomato purée
* 400g can chopped tomatoes
* 2 teaspoons dried Italian herbs
* 300ml (½ pint) hot beef stock
* 1 tablespoon gravy granules (optional)
* 200g (7oz) penne pasta

FOR THE SAUCE

* 60g (2oz) butter
* 60g (2oz) plain flour
* 450ml (¾ pint) semi-skimmed milk
* 60g (2oz) mature Cheddar cheese, grated
* 2 litre (3½ pint) ovenproof dish

1 Heat the oil in a large frying pan, add the onion and fry over a medium heat for 3 minutes, until softened. Turn the heat to high, add the garlic, mince and aubergine and fry for 5 minutes to brown them. Add the purée, tomatoes, all herbs and stock, bring to the boil and simmer for 25 minutes, until the beef is tender. Add gravy granules to thicken, if you like.

2 Set the oven to 200°C or Gas Mark 6. Meanwhile, cook the pasta in boiling water according to the packet instructions, then drain and set aside.

3 **To make the white sauce:** Put the butter, flour and milk into a large jug. Microwave on High for 4 minutes, stirring twice, until the sauce has boiled and thickened.

4 Stir the pasta into the meat mixture. Spoon into the dish. Pour on the sauce, sprinkle with the cheese and bake for 20 minutes, until golden.

TIP FROM OUR KITCHEN
If the sauce goes lumpy, whizz everything together with a stick blender.

Viva Las Vegas

Mike is good for me. He's full of surprises. This trip was a surprise — it had to be or I'd never have got here

I've been seeing Elvis a lot lately. It's becoming a regular occurrence and we've only been here two days.

"Look, there he is again," says Mike, holding his coffee cup out in Elvis's general direction. "Look at the rhinestones in that cat suit. Amazing, isn't it?"

I nod in agreement. Some things just take your breath away. "I wonder how long they took to sew on," I say idly.

"And I wonder if he did them or if his poor wife sat making her fingers sore."

"Stop thinking, just enjoy," says Mike. So I lean back and watch.

Don't worry, we're not those deluded souls who think Elvis never died. We're in Las Vegas. Gambling capital of the world.

It was Mike's idea. It usually is. One of his long-held dreams, he said, as he handed me the tickets.

"I never knew that," I said poring over the brochure for the hotel. I couldn't recall him saying anything about it before.

"There's a lot you don't know about me, Moneypenny." He wiggled his eyebrows, trying to look seductive. It didn't work. He just made me laugh. That's why I like being with him.

I watch Elvis swagger through the hotel lobby, then return to my cappuccino, stirring the chocolate into the frothy top. It's so different being with Mike, living in the moment instead of dwelling on the past. A past that included chocolates and flowers — and lots of them, guilty tokens of infidelity. I sip my coffee, drinking away the memories.

Mike pays the bill, leaves a tip, and we walk to the windowless casino where it's always night.

He passes me a handful of quarters. "Fancy a go?"

I shrug. I'm not a gambler.

"Go on. You should try everything once. Be a devil."

He stands by me as I slip the coins into the slot but the money is soon gone.

"Like it?" he asks, smiling.

"Not really. It's a bit mindless."

"At least you had a go, Jess." He puts his arm about my shoulder.

Mike is good for me. I don't get a chance to be a wallflower any more.

'Go on. You should try everything once'

He makes me do things I would never dream of and is full of surprises.

This trip was a surprise. It had to be or I'd never have got here. I'd have found so many excuses not to come. But Mike had organised it in fine detail — apart from the Elvis convention. He didn't know about that.

"It's like being in a parallel universe," I say, as we see Elvis at every turn. Fat Elvis, thin Elvis, Chinese Elvis, tall and short Elvis.

Las Vegas is nothing like you see on the telly. It's a surreal place. As soon as you land and walk through the airport there are machines lining the walkways, and it never ends.

"Where to next?" I ask and we walk out into the desert air. It's hot but breezy. Limousines glide up the strip and lights glitter.

"Lets just walk," he says.

I link my arm around his waist and we take in the spectacle that is Las Vegas in all its tacky, over-the-top glory.

"Don't you want to gamble, throw a few dice?" I ask.

Mike seems distracted by signs on the buildings as we walk along.

"It's not really my scene, Jess," he says quietly.

I look up at him; his cheek is twitching nervously.

"I thought Las Vegas was a dream. I thought you wanted to gamble."

He is quiet for a moment. Serious. Mike doesn't do serious.

"This is all the gambling I'm going to do, Jess." He stops on the pavement outside the Elvis Wedding Chapel. I can see lights flashing inside and an organ is playing *Love Me Tender*.

He leads me inside and we meet another Elvis. This one is a really good lookalike. He starts singing *It's Now Or Never*.

"It's all booked. If you want to." He produces a gold band from his inside pocket and takes my hand. "Don't think about it, Jess. Just do it."

I feel my breath leak from my toes, my fingers. I feel the blood rushing around like a locomotive.

"Do you love me?" Mike's voice is firm. Steady.

"Of course," I reply quickly. I never have to think about that.

"Life's a gamble, Jess," he says. "The winner takes it all."

"That's Abba, not Elvis." I giggle and the tension leaves my body. Mike makes me laugh. And that's the most important thing. No guilty flowers or chocolates, only seemingly impromptu flights to Vegas, a spontaneous walk along the strip.

"Marry me, Jess," He holds out the ring. *"Because I can't help.… falling in love with yoooouuuu."* He distorts his lips and thrusts his hips like the King himself.

Happiness bubbles inside me and I say yes. Marriage to Mike would never be a gamble — it's a dead cert.

THE END

© Francine Lee

17 Monday

18 Tuesday

19 Wednesday

20 Thursday

21 Friday

22 Saturday

23 Sunday

WORDSEARCH

Find all the listed items connected with Sherlock Holmes in the grid except one — they run either forwards or backwards, horizontally, vertically or diagonally, but always in a straight, unbroken line. The missing word is your answer.

```
S E M L O H K C O L R E H S J
S Z R E K L A T S R E E D I Y
S S C O T L A N D Y A R D R T
A M A Z A R I N S T O N E A R
L N O S D U H S R M Y I N R A
G O A P P I P E F R N O K T I
G I V R B V D P A T S N H H R
N T I A O R I T E G O C H U O
I C O A U M N L E W A B T R M
Y U L M K E L R L B P W C C R
F D I W M I G E N A E E E O O
I E N E G S D E N E I L P N S
N D L E A G H C D O O N S A S
G E N I E C O S L G L F U N E
A T B A I A U F I U I O S D F
M O B E V I T C E T E D C O O
T L R E T N O T E B O O K Y R
E N O S T A W N H O J R D L P
A S T U D Y I N S C A R L E T
```

A STUDY IN SCARLET
BASKERVILLE
CLUE
COLONEL MORAN
DEDUCTION
DEERSTALKER
DETECTIVE
DR JOHN WATSON
ELEMENTARY
FOG

INTELLIGENT
KNOWLEDGEABLE
LOGIC
MAGNIFYING GLASS
MAZARIN STONE
MRS HUDSON
MURDER
NOTEBOOK
PIPE
PROFESSOR MORIARTY

REICHENBACH
SCOTLAND YARD
SHERLOCK HOLMES
SIR ARTHUR CONAN DOYLE
SUSPECT
TOBIAS GREGSON
TWEED SUIT
VILLAIN
VIOLIN

CODEWORD

Codeword grid with given letters L, E, A at top and the key showing 1 = A, 10 = L, 22 = E.

Alphabet key: A̶ B C D E̶ F G H I J K L̶ M N O P Q R S T U V W X Y Z

1	2	3	4	5	6	7	8	9	10	11	12	13
A									L			

14	15	16	17	18	19	20	21	22	23	24	25	26
								E				

Solutions to this month's puzzle on next month's puzzle

SOLUTIONS OCTOBER, 2014

ACROSS: 1 Anaesthetic **8** Miser **9** Negligees **11** Nursemaids **12** Zinc **14** Camps **16** Ill-gotten **18** Lend an ear **20** Lisps **22** Ugly **23** Picnicking **27** Elopement **28** Cadet **29** Synthesiser
DOWN: 2 Nostrum **3** Eerie **4** Tentative **5** Egged **6** Ixia **7** Demist **8** Monoculture **10** Second sight **13** Fowl **15** Scan **17** Lorgnette **19** Nelson **21** Spindle **24** Inert **25** Cacti **26** Deny

24 Monday

25 Tuesday

26 Wednesday

27 Thursday

28 Friday

29 Saturday

30 Sunday

DECEMBER

Stollen x

1 Monday

2 Tuesday

3 Wednesday

4 Thursday

5 Friday

6 Saturday

7 Sunday

Celebration Stöllen

SERVES 12
CALORIES 300
FAT 11g
SATURATED FAT 4.5g
SUITABLE FOR FREEZING Yes

INGREDIENTS

* 325g (11oz) strong white bread flour
* 7g sachet easy-blend yeast
* 45g (1½oz) golden caster sugar
* 1 medium egg, lightly beaten
* 45g (1½oz) butter, melted
* 100ml (3½fl oz) warm milk
* 250g (8oz) soft dried apricots, chopped
* 4 tablespoons orange liqueur
* 100g (3½oz) pistachios
* 60g (2oz) dried cranberries
* 100g (3½oz) white chocolate, chopped
* 2 teaspoons icing sugar, to dust

1 Put the flour, yeast and sugar into a bowl. Add the egg, melted butter and milk. Knead together on a lightly floured surface by hand for 10 minutes or with a dough hook in an electric mixer for 5 minutes, until smooth and elastic. Put into a greased bowl, cover with cling film and leave in a warm place for about 1 hour until doubled in size.

2 Put apricots into a pan with the orange liqueur. Warm through for 2 minutes, then put into a bowl to cool. Whizz the pistachios in a blender until finely ground. Add the cranberries, white chocolate, apricots and liqueur. Whizz again to combine.

3 Turn out the mixture on to a sheet of baking parchment and shape into a log about 25cm (10in) long. Pop in the freezer for 5-10 minutes, to firm up.

4 Roll out the bread dough on a lightly floured surface to 28 x 18cm (11 x 7in). Place the apricot and pistachio log on top, slightly to the left of the centre.

5 Brush the left-hand edge with water. Fold the right-hand side of dough over the apricot filling and press edge down firmly, to seal. Cover loosely with cling film and leave in a warm place to rise for 30 minutes. Set the oven to 190°C or Gas Mark 5.

6 Remove the cling film, and then bake the stöllen for 25 minutes until risen and golden. Cool on a wire rack. Dust with icing sugar. Slice to serve.

* For freezing, don't dust with the icing sugar. When cold, wrap well in a freezer bag and freeze for up to 3 months. Allow to defrost, then dust with icing sugar before serving.

POST – CARD

Lough Gur in County Limerick, Ireland

Reader Susie Kearley, from Princes Risborough in Buckinghamshire, chooses Lough Gur, in County Limerick, Ireland

'On our holidays, we often return to Lough Gur, as it's the most wonderfully tranquil place. There is an ancient stone circle at the edge of the lake, and you can imagine why our pagan ancestors would have enjoyed a place like this — you really do feel at one with nature here. There's also a visitor centre and exhibition that tells you a little about the history of this gorgeous spot.'

POST – CARD

Reader Susan Rodger, from Sawtry in Cambridgeshire, nominates Calgary, which lies east of the Rocky Mountains, in Alberta, Canada

Calgary in Alberta, Canada

'Compact and clean, you can use the C-train to travel free around the centre of Calgary. The Glenbow Museum is fascinating, the Christmas parade magical, and there are wonderful parks and plazas bursting with flowers. The dragon boat races on the Bow River are worth watching, but the Calgary Stampede (left) is unforgettable, as the whole city goes cowboy crazy.'

8 Monday

9 Tuesday

10 Wednesday

11 Thursday

12 Friday

13 Saturday

14 Sunday

Fun Presents To Make

We've come up with great ways to use up remnants of fabric, felt and left-over wool to create an array of cute Christmas gifts

MATERIALS

1 x 50g ball of Rico Solo DK in each of Red (006) and White (001). Yarn costs about £2 per 50g ball. A pair of 3¾mm (No. 9) knitting needles. Brooch fastener or safety pin.

TENSION

23 stitches and 45 rows, to 10 x 10cm, over garter stitch, using 3¾mm needles.

ABBREVIATIONS

K, knit; st, stitch; tog, together; dec, decrease; sl, slip; gst, garter st (every row k); psso, pass sl st over; skpo, (sl1, k1, psso); up1, pick up loop lying between needles and k into the back of it.

NOTE

Yarn amounts are based on average requirements and are therefore approximate. Instructions in square brackets are worked as stated after 2nd bracket.

Colourful Corsage

PETALS (MAKE 6)

With 3¾mm needles and Red, cast on 11 sts. K 2 rows.
1st increase row: K1, [up1, k4, up1, k1] twice — 15 sts. K 1 row.
2nd increase row: K1, [up1, k6, up1, k1] twice — 19 sts. K 1 row.
3rd increase row: K1, [up1, k8, up1, k1] twice — 23 sts. K 1 row.
4th increase row: K1, [up1, k10, up1, k1] twice — 27 sts. K 7 rows.
1st dec row: K5, k2tog, skpo, k9, k2tog, skpo, k5 — 23 sts. K 3 rows.
2nd dec row: K4, k2tog, skpo, k7, k2tog, skpo, k4 — 19 sts. K 3 rows.
3rd dec row: K3, k2tog, skpo, k5, k2tog, skpo, k3 — 15 sts. K 1 row.
4th dec row: K2, k2tog, skpo, k3, k2tog, skpo, k2 — 11 sts. K 1 row.
5th dec row: K1, [k2tog, skpo, k1] twice — 7 sts. K 1 row.
6th dec row: K2tog, sl1, k2tog, psso, skpo — 3 sts. K 1 row. Cast off.

CENTRE

With 3¾mm needles and White, cast on 24 sts. K 15 rows. Cast off.

TO MAKE UP

Join row-ends together on each petal, leaving cast-on edge open. With seam at centre back, oversew cast-on edge, then fold cast-on edge in half and secure in position for base of petal.
With two strands of Red yarn, run

a gathering thread through base of petals, pull up tightly until all ends meet up at centre of flower and secure in position. Join petals together by working a couple of stitches just below 1st decrease row. Roll centre from cast-on edge to cast-off edge and secure in position. Wind rolled centre in a spiral motion to form a disc and secure in position. Stitch disc to centre of flower. If used, attach brooch fastener to back of flower.

Time For Tea

SIDES (MAKE 2)

Lining: With 5½mm needles and Red, cast on 9 sts for top edge.

1st inc row: [Inc kwise in next st] 8 times, k1 — 17 sts. P 1 row.

2nd inc row: K1, [inc in next st, k1] 8 times — 25 sts. P 1 row.

3rd inc row: K1, [inc in next st, k2] 8 times — 33 sts. Ss 3 rows.

4th inc row: K1, [inc in next st, k3] 8 times — 41 sts. Ss 40 rows. K 1 row for fold line.

Top layer: Increase row: K5, [up1, k6] 6 times — 47 sts. P 1 row.

Stranding yarn not in use loosely across wrong side and reading chart (see right) from right to left on right side (k) rows and from left to right on wrong side (p) rows, work in ss and pattern from chart until 38th row of chart has been worked.

1st dec row: With Red, k2, [k2tog, k3] 9 times — 38 sts. With Ecru, p 1 row.

Next row: K2 Ecru, [1 Red, 2 Ecru] to end.

2nd dec row: With Ecru, p2tog, [p1, p2tog] 12 times — 25 sts. With Red, k 1 row.

3rd dec row: P1 Ecru, [2 Red, with Ecru p2tog] 6 times — 19 sts.

Next row: K1 Red, [1 Ecru, 3 Red, 1 Ecru, 1 Red] 3 times.

4th dec row: P2 Red, [with Ecru p3tog, p3 Red] twice, with Ecru p3tog, p2 Red — 13 sts.

5th dec row: With Red, k2tog, [k1, k3tog] twice, k1, k2tog — 7 sts. Cast off.

CORD

With 4mm needles and Red, cast on 6 sts. Ss 60 rows. Cast off.

TIE

With 4mm needles and Red, cast on 10 sts. Cast off.

TO MAKE UP

Join top layers along cast-off edge and sides to fold line, leaving openings at each side for spout and handle. Now, join lining together, leaving openings to match top layer. Push lining inside then join top layer and lining together on each side of openings. Join ends of cord to form a ring. Twist ring into figure 8, thus forming a bow. Place tie over centre of bow and join short ends together. Sew bow to top of cosy, sewing through both layers.

MEASUREMENTS

Width 24cm/9½in.
Height 19cm/7½in.

MATERIALS

2 x 50g balls of Rico Essentials Soft Merino Aran in Red (08) and 1 ball in Ecru (60). Yarn costs about £3.50 per 50g ball. A pair of 5½mm (No. 5) and 4mm (No. 8) knitting needles.

TENSION

18 stitches and 24 rows, to 10 x 10cm, over stocking stitch, using 5½mm needles. 14 stitches and 22 rows, to 10 x 10cm, over pattern, using 5½mm needles.

ABBREVIATIONS

***K,** knit; **p,** purl; **st,** stitch; **tog,** together; **dec,** decrease; **inc,** increase (by working twice in same st); **ss,** stocking st (k on right side and p on wrong side); **up1,** pick up loop lying between needles and k into the back of it.*

NOTE

Yarn amounts are based on average requirements and are approximate. Instructions in square brackets are worked as stated after 2nd bracket.

47 STITCHES

Your Good Health

Ask Dr Mel

Q My GP has prescribed omeprazole because I need to take ibuprofen every day for my osteoarthritis pain. Is it safe? Should I have breaks from it, or tests?

A Non-steroidal anti-inflammatory drugs (NSAIDs) such as ibuprofen can cause stomach ulceration and bleeding, especially in older people or when taken with other drugs that irritate the stomach, including antidepressants such as Prozac.

Proton-pump inhibitors (PPIs) such as omeprazole reduce acid production, and are used to to protect the stomach against NSAIDs in people at higher risk, as well as to treat ulcers, heartburn and acid reflux. In addition to the side-effects listed in PPI patient information leaflets, recent research suggests that suppressing your stomach acid could make you more prone to the severe diarrhoea caused by Clostridium difficile bacteria, and that smokers who take PPIs long-term may be more likely to fracture their hips. But, as always with medication, your GP can help you to balance the potential benefits and risks. People taking long-term PPIs for reflux are now recommended to take them only when needed, rather than every day, but in your case, you could consider taking a non-NSAID painkiller instead, so that you don't need to take a daily PPI.

TRY THIS) Yoga

Some gentle yoga the morning after the night before will help you relax. Yoga teacher Sybille Gebhardt suggests a half shoulder-stand. "It helps cleanse the lymphatic system and reduces blood pressure," she says. Lie on a mat on your back, legs together, arms by sides, palms facing the floor. Place a cushion under your tailbone. Breathe in and raise your legs, keeping them straight with feet flexed. Breathe in again as you gently lift your hips, pressing your arms into the floor for support. Hold for half a minute, building up to three

HEALTH ON MY SHELF
Judi James, behavioural body and language expert

What's in your medicine cabinet?
Bite and sting cream and two night creams I never use, as they bring me out in spots!

What's good in your fridge?
Everything. I'm a vegetarian. Fruit, veg, yogurt; big spuds, as I love jacket potatoes.

What's your favourite exercise?
Rushing and fidgeting; I rarely keep still! I love swimming and dancing.

What's a special foodie treat?
On Christmas Day, I have a jacket potato with caviar on top. I read that Jackie Kennedy ate this, so it feels glamorous.

How do you cope with stress?
I can usually see the funny side of things.

If you can't sleep, what helps?
I do a version of counting sheep that involves planning a plot for a new TV soap.

Any good childhood remedies?
Arnica gel. My mum used it when I fell over. Just rubbing it in makes you feel better!

TAKE 5...
Reasons To Seek Immediate Medical Advice

1 TIGHT OR HEAVY PAIN at the front of the chest, especially if it spreads to the arm or neck, or makes you feel faint, breathless or sweaty.

2 CHOKING or severe/ unexplained difficulty in breathing.

3 VOMITING/COUGHING UP BLOOD, jet black stools, or bleeding that is heavy or won't stop.

4 POSSIBLE MENINGITIS — headache, fever, neck stiffness, sensitivity to light, limb pain, confusion and/or a rash that won't disappear when pressed with a glass.

5 SUDDEN FACIAL, arm or leg weakness and/or slurred speech.

15 Monday

16 Tuesday

17 Wednesday

18 Thursday

19 Friday

20 Saturday

21 Sunday

My Best Friend

What dare-devil profession would Robbie Blake grow into? Would I always be along for the ride, half-scared and half-thrilled?

I gaze at the clock. Quarter to three. Time to get my skates on and assume my position at the school gates. I smile, thinking of the first time Mickey ran out and saw me there. "Mum!" he'd said in a tone of horror. "I'm not in infants now. You can't do this to me."

Luckily for me, it turned out his mate Leo's mum was a bigger embarrassment. She worked at the school three days a week as a dinner lady.

Today isn't just any old day at the school gates, though. Today is the anniversary of Robbie's death.

It's best to be out and about on a day like this, I tell myself, crossing briskly to the red-bricked playground in the shadow of lime trees and a busy A-road.

I wonder how many people — apart from his parents, and his sister Lu, who I see from time to time — still think of Robbie.

He would have loved the new equipment they've put in the playground. All the parents clubbed together to buy the brightly coloured play-safe gear for small, explorative feet to scramble over. It made me sad for Robbie, the day it was officially opened. He would have enjoyed test-riding it all, kid that he was. That's how we met, if you ignore the fact we were already in the same class.

The old slide that used to stand in the playground had been high and excitingly slippery, its metal struts grounded in concrete instead of the butter-soft rubber favoured today. I was halfway down the slide one break-time when my raspberry pink woolly tights snagged on the sides and I stuck fast — only to hear a sharp cry of annoyed distress behind me, and feel a solid object butt me free and send me flying off the end on to the hard ground. Luckily, I landed on my bottom, well padded by those thick tights.

Robbie could have been less lucky, as he had flown down the slide red head first, ignoring the posted strictures against such manoeuvres. As it was, he landed sharply on his knee instead.

He managed to grin through his pain. He liked being the centre of

The kids stream out on cue, at half-three. No sign of Mickey

attention and I liked him for being at ease with it, since I was the opposite; come the school nativity play, I lived in dread of promotion beyond my natural limits as a (non-baaing) sheep.

Robbie was always the inn-keeper. One year, he told Mary and Joseph they could have the stable, but it didn't include the early-bird breakfast, so in the morning, they'd have to go across the road for an Egg McMuffin.

I'd always known he'd do great things in life — and somehow I saw myself included. What dare-devil profession would Robert Blake grow into? Would I always be along for the ride, clutching his coat-tails, half-scared and half-thrilled?

I know now that you can't live your life vicariously through other people, but it wasn't like that with Robbie. Although I would never be an extrovert, I drew enough inspiration from him to go head-first down the slide myself after a while. We were unlikely friends at the start — but, perhaps because of that, the best of friends.

The kids stream out on cue, at half-three. No sign of Mickey. He's got judo club tonight, and Bobbi — short for Roberta — is already at "big" school. How time flies!

There's always one straggler at the school gates. Today it's a small, tow-haired boy with trailing laces and a school bag bigger than himself. New to the school, I think. I haven't seen him before and it explains why he's alone, no mates as yet to hang around with, swapping football cards.

He looks lost and forlorn, but then I see a woman wave from the parked cars across the road and feel relieved that his lift is watching out for him.

'All set?' I smile.

To my surprise, he slips a sticky hand into mine. Some of the kids don't like to, especially the boys. Just before we reach safety, he turns and smiles and, in the half-creased sunlight, I catch a flash of red hair, a wide grin. "Thanks," he says. "You're an ace lollipop lady. For a girl."

As he runs off, I realise I imagined that last line.

Of course, in my day, we used to walk home, the older ones keeping tabs on the younger, both the crossing and the A-road being later innovations. But even then, the road claimed its victims...

As with the playground equipment, we parents had banded together and campaigned for a lollipop lady on the crossing, once we realised kids would be running heedlessly across the road to and from the phalanx of parked cars.

When I volunteered, I was thinking of the safety of my own kids, but I was thinking of him as well. Of the fearless and big-hearted best friend I had at eight. My best friend who will always be eight.

THE END
© Gabrielle Mullarkey

22 Monday

23 Tuesday

24 Wednesday

25 Thursday CHRISTMAS DAY

26 Friday BOXING DAY

27 Saturday

28 Sunday

CROSSWORD

Read down the letters in the shaded squares to spell out an indoor game (7)

ACROSS

12 Interest-paying bank service (7,7)
13 Large-scale disruption (8)
14 Elegant, stylish (4)
15 Renting a room (7)
16 Wonderful! (10)
17 Room at the top of a house (5)
19 Deep or intense sorrow (5)
20 Throbs, thumps (6)
22 Unable to hear (4)
25 Devastated by armed conflict (3-4)
26 In the nick of time (2,3,4,6)
29 White nocturnal bird of prey (5,3)
30 Immobile, motionless (6)
31 Neat, well-dressed (5)
34 Take away, extract (6)
36 Most warm-hearted (9)
38 Having happened lately (6)
39 Bid (5)
40 Terminology of a profession (6)
41 Natural impulse in animals (8)
45 Piece of paper often enclosed with posted brochures (11,4)
46 On-air debate with the public (5-2)
47 Remain as a guest (4)
48 Christian festival often in April (6)
50 Opposite of 'fresh' (5)
52 Fury (5)
55 Spread around (10)
58 Pierce ___, actor who played James Bond (7)
59 Shelf for spice bottles (4)
61 Areas prepared for young plants (8)
62 Punctuation marks used to indicate direct speech (8,6)

DOWN

1 Blow from a whip (4)
2 Place to keep cookies (7,3)
3 Nimble, sprightly (5)
4 Prison guard (6)
5 Happening by chance (10)
6 Sudden forward thrust of the body (5)
7 Thing on a list (4)
8 Uncompetitive race (3,3)
9 Trio of people (9)
10 Enclosed shopping precinct (4)
11 Producing articles on a large scale (13)
18 Flat carrying-dish (4)
21 Away from work, vacationing (2,5)
22 Forceful, energetic (7)
23 Fishing boat (7)
24 Spooky quality (11)
27 Fastest (8)
28 Colleague (8)
32 Having its own kitchen and bathroom (4-9)
33 Transport of goods in containers (7)
35 Reward too highly (7)
37 Loose dress worn in bed (7)
41 Card with a TV or film script attached, to aid a speaker (5,5)
42 Puzzles, riddles (10)
43 Football pitch boundaries (9)
44 Actually being performed at the time of viewing (4)
49 Fruit cordial (6)
51 Hang about (6)
53 In a higher position (5)
54 Strike (a door) (5)
56 Ebb and flow of the sea (4)
57 Give out (radiation, eg) (4)
60 Steep rugged rock or cliff (4)
53 Marking (envelopes) (8)
54 Advancing very slowly (7)
55 Vehicles licensed to carry passengers for payment (8)
57 Melodious birds (5)
60 Warning gestures or sounds (7)
61 Full of bravado (4-2)
65 Livid (5)
66 Silly row (4)
68 Score of nothing in sport (3)
69 Sort, type (3)

Solutions to this month's puzzle on JANUARY 2014 puzzle

SOLUTIONS NOVEMBER, 2014

BASKERVILLE

29 Monday

30 Tuesday

31 Wednesday

1 Jan, 2015 NEW YEAR'S DAY

2 Jan, 2015

3 Jan, 2015

4 Jan, 2015

Woman's Weekly Yearbook 2014

Visit **Pedigreebooks.com** to find out more on this year's **Woman's Weekly** Yearbook, scan with your mobile device to learn more.

Visit www.pedigreebooks.com

Pedigree Books, Beech Hill House, Walnut Gardens, Exeter EX4 4DH